Cooking with
LOVE
&
CEREAL

Cooking with LOVE & CEREAL

Betty McMichael
with Karen McDonald

Christian Herald Books
40 Overlook Drive, Chappaqua, New York 10514

Dedicated
to
the memory of Scott Alan Collins,
the authors' grandson and cousin,
January 11, 1969 – February 3, 1971

Scripture quotations, unless otherwise identified or included in quotations
from other authors, are from the New American Standard Bible, © The Lockman
Foundation 1960, 1962, 1963, 1968, 1971, 1972, 1973, 1975.

Library of Congress Cataloging in Publication Data
McMichael, Betty.
    Cooking with love 'n cereal.

    Includes bibliographical references and index.
    1. Cookery (Cereals)   I. McDonald, Karen, joint
author.   II. Title.
TX808.M28   641.6   80-69312
ISBN 0-915684-80-2

First Edition
CHRISTIAN HERALD BOOKS, 40 Overlook Drive,
Chappaqua, New York 10514
Printed in the United States of America

Contents

Preface

My husband and I enjoy doing things with our grandchildren. Whenever possible, we like to spend time with each one alone, because that way we can get better acquainted with them as individuals. Knowing them better gives us clues about how we can help each one best. As we work and play together, we sometimes find opportunities to discuss with them the things God has called to our attention over the years.

Doing things together benefits us just as much as it does our grandchildren. We learn from them, and our lives are greatly enriched as we have a part in theirs. Our grandchildren are sometimes surprised to discover, as they come to know us better, that we are real people with real problems, but also with real love and understanding.

Although we are far from being perfect examples, we know that our grandchildren observe and sometimes copy our actions and reactions. They are constant reminders to us of the truth of Abraham Lincoln's words: "There is just one way to bring up a child in the way he should go, and that is to travel that way yourself."

Many influences contribute to a child's training. Bible teaching at home and church is important. Prayer for and with a child has a strong impact. But unless teaching and praying are accompanied by examples of Christian living, the child is not apt to incorporate his parents' and grandparents' spiritual values into his own life.

Grandparents in some cultures are assigned primary responsibility for child care. This is not true in America, nor do many American grandparents wish for it to be the case. However, grandparents in our culture have many opportunities to influence their grandchildren. That will be increasingly true as people live longer and grandparents make up an ever larger percentage of the total population.

In our desire to help grandchildren, it is important that we not usurp the rights and responsibilities of parents. Ideally, the grandparent role is one of supporting and strengthening the authority and guidance of parents. One of the best ways of doing this is by informally communicating spiritual values while doing things with our grandchildren.

Cooking is one of the things grandparents often enjoy doing with their grandchildren. It is a good way to have fun while getting to know each other better and at the same time contributing to the well-being and enjoyment of others.

My granddaughter Karen and I have worked together to bring you this special collection of recipes. One of the first recipes we ever prepared together was a simple treat made with a breakfast cereal. Since then we have enjoyed finding out what else could be made with various kinds of breakfast foods as ingredients. The recipes, of course, can be used by anyone, cooking alone or with a partner. Parents can use them in cooking with their children. But we hope some other grandparents and grandchildren will enjoy preparing these foods together.

We have inserted among our recipes many quotations meant to remind us of the importance of the kind of example those of the older generation set before the younger ones. We appreciate the use of these brief quotations from various sources, of which the most frequently cited are acknowledged to the best of our ability in the Acknowledgments. In places where no author is named, it is because we have been unable to determine authorship.

One of the special blessings we received in preparing this book was in having parents and grandparents who helped test recipes report spiritual benefits from cooking with their children or grandchildren. Some told of developing a rapport that had been lacking for some time. Their comments encouraged us to believe that God can and will use as simple an idea as cooking together with breakfast cereals to bring enjoyment and spiritual growth to some of His children of all ages.

Betty McMichael

Grandma and I always liked to cook when I was littler. But two years ago, we started talking about making a cookbook. I was ten years old then. We collected three different kinds of recipes — peanut butter, oatmeal, and breakfast cereal. While saving all these recipes, we decided we would do a cereal cookbook. We put the others aside and collected more cereal recipes.

I pasted recipes on sheets of notebook paper. Both of us organized them. We had almost a thousand. We gave them names and put numbers on them according to whether they were cookies, breads, candies, meats, or other foods. Grandma used those recipes for ideas and wrote new ones. One of Grandma's friends typed them for us. Afterward we started testing the recipes.

We couldn't do a thousand recipes by ourselves. We needed some help, so we got some other people to volunteer. We handed ten recipes to each team. Some were grandmas and granddaughters, just as we are. Some were mothers and children. An adult and a child always worked together. Both girls and boys helped. My brother Kurt helped a lot. He and I cooked at home with Mom and at Grandma's almost every time we went there.

We asked the teams to fill out a rating sheet for each recipe. They told how well they liked the food, how easy the directions were to follow, and what changes should be made. We also asked them to give us a sample so we could see if we liked it. Sometimes we didn't like it at all! One time, everyone laughed when I said we should put a warning on one recipe that it is "not recommended for dentures — or teeth." But instead we crossed it off the list of ones to use.

Both Grandma and I got tired of cooking sometimes. But we didin't mind eating! Finally, the recipes were all tested. We picked about 300 to put in our cookbook.

Grandparents don't just cook with their grandchildren but do other fun things, too. For instance, I like fishing with Grandpa. I like to help him build things and learn to play the accordion. There are other fun things to do. It's nice to listen to them talk about living on the farm and making taffy with their moms and grandmas.

Karen McDonald, age twelve

Acknowledgments

We thank the Lockman Foundation for permission to quote from the *New American Standard Bible*. Copyright information on the edition used is given on the copyright page.

We gratefully acknowledge the generosity and help of breakfast cereal companies who supplied ideas for many of our recipes and permission to use their registered trademarks. These companies and trademarks named in our recipes are as follows:

General Foods Corporation — POST® GRAPE-NUTS® brand cereal and POST® GRAPE-NUTS® FLAKES.

General Mills, Inc. — CHEERIOS® breakfast cereal, GOLDEN GRAHAMS® breakfast cereal, KIX® breakfast cereal, and WHEATIES® breakfast cereal.

Kellogg Company — KELLOGG's®, ALL-BRAN®, APPLE JACKS®, BRAN BUDS®, COCOA KRISPIES®, CRACKLIN' BRAN®, FROOT LOOPS®, PRODUCT 19®, RICE KRISPIES®, and SPECIAL K®.

The Quaker Oats Company — CAP'N CRUNCH®.

Ralston Purina Company — BRAN CHEX® cereal, CORN CHEX® cereal, RICE CHEX® cereal, and WHEAT CHEX® cereal.

Our thanks go to all who have helped make this book a reality. We appreciate the work of Leslie Stobbe and his editorial staff at Christian Herald Books. Special thanks go to Arlene Culbertson, who did all the manuscript typing and, with her twelve-year-old son, more than her fair share of recipe testing.

Children who worked with a parent, grandparent, or some other adult in testing our recipes were: Vicki Collins, Ken Culbertson, Patty DeFore, Kristina Easter, Colin Faulkner, Susan Hillabush, Ken and Randy Hubin, Ann Lundberg, Kurt McDonald, Sarah McNutt, Sharilyn Mullet, Tracy Newton, Paula Olson, Kathy and Tami Patrick, Rebecca Pfaff, David and Mary Plank, Jolene Reed, Liza and Michael Rinehart, Lance and Libbie Simpson, Gladys Tsao-Wu, Michelle Wallick, Karen Werthman, and Julie Williams.

Quotations on pages 65, 67, 132, 137, and 173 are from *Thoughts for Young Mothers* by Elsie D. Holsinger, copyright 1953. Moody Bible Institute of Chicago, Moody Press. Used by permission.

Quotations on pages 18, 172, 176, 184, and 212 are from *A Mother's Wages* by Elizabeth Walker Strachan, copyright 1957. Moody Bible Institute of Chicago, Moody Press. Used by permission.

Quotations on pages 64, 73, 80, and 82 are from *A Plate of Hot Toast* by Jeanette Lockerbie, copyright 1971. Moody Bible Institute of Chicago, Moody Press. Used by permission.

Poem, "A Child's Heart," on page 215 by Wanda Sturgill Vail is used by permission.

We also thank Don Bender for the fine artwork in this book.

1
Breads

DATE-BRAN MUFFINS

       1 **cup sifted all-purpose flour**
       3 **teaspoons baking powder**
       2 **tablespoons sugar**
     ¾ **teaspoon salt**
     ⅓ **cup shortening**
       1 **well-beaten egg**
     ¾ **cup milk**
    1¼ **cups bran flakes**
     ½ **cup chopped dates**

1. Combine sifted flour, baking powder, sugar, and salt.
    Sift together.
2. Cut shortening into flour mixture with 2 knives or
    a pastry blender.
3. Mix beaten egg and milk. Add to flour mixture, stirring
    just until dry ingredients are moist.
4. Gently stir in cereal and dates.
5. Spoon into muffin cups, filling each about ⅔ full. Bake
    at 400°F. about 20 minutes. Makes about 10 muffins.

One generation shall praise Thy works to another,
And shall declare Thy mighty acts.   PSALM 145:4

GRAPE-NUTS MUFFINS

    1 **cup sifted all-purpose flour**
    2 **tablespoons sugar**
    2 **teaspoons baking powder**
   ¾ **teaspoon salt**
   ⅓ **cup shortening**
   ¾ **cup milk**
    1 **well-beaten egg**
1¼ **cups POST GRAPE-NUTS FLAKES**

1. Sift together flour, sugar, baking powder, and salt.
2. Cut in shortening.
3. Add milk and beaten egg. Mix just enough to moisten dry ingredients.
4. Gently stir in cereal.
5. Spoon into greased muffin cups, filling each about ⅔ full. Bake at 400°F. about 20 minutes. Makes about 10 medium-size muffins.
   Variations: Add ½ cup prunes, dried apricots, or raisins.
   Add ⅓ cup crumbled, well-cooked bacon. Cut salt to ½ teaspoon.

HONEY-BRAN MUFFINS

1 **cup KELLOGG'S ALL-BRAN cereal**
1 **cup milk**
3 **tablespoons melted margarine**
¼ **cup honey**
1 **slightly beaten egg**
1 **cup all-purpose flour**
½ **teaspoon salt**
3 **teaspoons baking powder**

1. Combine cereal and milk in large bowl. Let stand 10 minutes.
2. In small bowl, beat margarine with honey until light and fluffy. Add slightly beaten egg. Mix well. Add to bran mixture and stir.
3. Add flour, salt, and baking powder.
4. Put in greased muffin cups, filling each about ½ full. Bake at 400°F. about 20 to 30 minutes. Makes 12 large muffins.

JAM-FILLED MUFFINS

   1¼ cups all-purpose flour
    3 teaspoons baking powder
    1 teaspoon salt
   ⅓ cup sugar
    2 cups cornflakes
    1 cup milk
    1 egg
   ⅓ cup softened margarine
   ¼ cup jam or preserves

1. Sift flour, baking powder, salt, and sugar into small bowl.
2. Put cereal into large bowl. Add milk and stir. Let stand until cereal softens, 2 or 3 minutes. Add egg and margarine and beat.
3. Add flour mixture, stirring just until dry ingredients are moistened.
4. Divide batter into 12 greased 2½ inch muffin cups. Indent center of each muffin. Fill with 1 teaspoon jam or preserves. Smooth small amount of batter over top. Bake at 400°F. about 25 minutes, until brown. Makes 12 large muffins.

MOLASSES MUFFINS

   1¼ cups all-purpose flour
    1 teaspoon baking powder
   ½ teaspoon baking soda
    1 teaspoon salt
    1 cup KELLOGG'S BRAN BUDS cereal
   ¾ cup milk
   ½ cup molasses
    1 egg
   ⅓ cup shortening
   ½ cup seedless raisins

1. Combine flour, baking powder, soda, and salt in small bowl.
2. Mix cereal, milk, and molasses in large bowl. Let stand about 2 minutes until cereal is soft.
3. Add egg and shortening. Beat well. Add raisins. Stir in flour mixture just until dry ingredients are moist.
4. Divide batter into 12 greased 2½ inch muffin cups. Bake at 400°F. about 15 minutes, until nicely browned. Makes 12 large muffins.

REFRIGERATOR MUFFINS

2 cups wheat biscuits
4 cups KELLOGG'S BRAN BUDS cereal
2 cups boiling water
3 cups sugar
1 cup shortening
4 beaten eggs
5 cups all-purpose flour
5 teaspoons baking soda
1 teaspoon salt
1 quart buttermilk

1. Mix cereals together in large saucepan. Pour boiling water over them and let soak a few minutes.
2. Cream sugar and shortening together in large bowl.
3. Combine beaten eggs, flour, soda, salt, and buttermilk. Add to creamed mixture. Blend well.
4. Add creamed mixture to soaked cereals. Stir.
5. Store covered in refrigerator up to 1 month. Bake as needed in greased muffin cups at 400°F. for 20 minutes. Makes 6 to 8 dozen.
   Variation: Cut recipe in half or quarter if none of batter is being refrigerated for later use.

A good man leaves an inheritance to his children's children.
PROVERBS 13:22

MAPLE MUFFINS

2 eggs
¾ cup maple-flavored syrup
2½ cups bran flakes, crushed
1 cup sour cream
1 cup all-purpose flour
1 teaspoon baking soda
½ cup chopped walnuts

1. Beat eggs with fork in medium-size bowl. Blend in syrup.
2. Add crushed cereal. Mix well. Let stand 5 minutes.
3. Add sour cream. Beat.
4. Stir in flour, soda, and nuts until flour is moist. Batter will still be lumpy.
5. Spoon into greased muffin cups. Bake at 400°F. 15 to 20 minutes, until light brown. Makes 12 large or 18 small muffins.

BANANA-BUTTERMILK MUFFINS

   1 **cup sifted all-purpose flour**
   2 **teaspoons baking powder**
  ½ **teaspoon baking soda**
  ¼ **teaspoon salt**
  ¼ **cup firmly packed brown sugar**
   1 **cup granola**
   3 **tablespoons vegetable oil**
   1 **beaten egg**
  ½ **cup buttermilk**
  ⅔ **cup mashed bananas**

1. Sift flour, baking powder, soda, and salt into bowl.
2. Mix in sugar and cereal.
3. Add oil, egg, buttermilk, and mashed bananas. Stir only until dry ingredients are moist.
4. Divide batter into 12 muffin cups, filling about ⅔ full. Bake at 425°F. about 15 minutes, until light brown. Makes 12 large muffins.

We must feed on the Bread of Life ourselves before we can serve it to others.   DENNIS J. DEHAAN

ORANGE-FLAVORED MUFFINS

 1⅔ **cups all-purpose flour**
  ½ **cup sugar**
   3 **teaspoons baking powder**
  ¾ **teaspoon salt**
   1 **cup POST GRAPE-NUTS brand cereal**
   2 **eggs**
  ¾ **cup orange juice**
  ½ **cup melted margarine**
   1 **tablespoon grated orange rind**

1. Combine flour, sugar, baking powder, and salt in large bowl. Stir in cereal.
2. In small bowl, beat eggs until thick. Add orange juice, margarine, and orange rind. Add to first mixture, mixing just enough to moisten dry ingredients.
3. Fill greased muffin cups about ⅔ full.
4. Bake at 425°F. for 12 to 14 minutes, until light brown. Serve warm. Makes 16 muffins.

CINNAMON-TOPPED PECAN MUFFINS
MUFFINS
1 cup all-purpose flour
2½ teaspoons baking powder
½ teaspoon salt
½ teaspoon nutmeg
¼ cup sugar
1 cup KELLOGG'S BRAN BUDS cereal
¾ cup milk
1 egg
¼ cup shortening
¾ cup finely chopped pecans
TOPPING
1 teaspoon cinnamon
⅓ cup sugar
¼ cup melted margarine

1. Combine flour, baking powder, salt, nutmeg, and ¼ cup sugar.
2. Stir together cereal and milk in large bowl. Let stand about 1 minute, until cereal is softened. Beat in egg and shortening. Add pecans and stir.
3. Add flour mixture to cereal mixture all at once. Mix only until dry ingredients are moist.
4. Spoon batter into greased muffin cups, filling each about ⅔ full. Bake at 400°F. about 15 minutes. Take out of pans.
5. Combine cinnamon and ⅓ cup sugar. Dip tops of hot muffins into melted margarine and then into cinnamon mixture. Serve warm. Makes 12.

It would be impossible to enumerate the daily joys that come from having a part in the growth of a child.   ELIZABETH WALKER STRACHAN

YOGURT MUFFINS

    1 **cup wheat biscuits**
    1 **cup plain yogurt**
  1⅓ **cups unsifted all-purpose flour**
   ½ **cup shredded sharp cheddar cheese**
  1½ **teaspoons baking powder**
   ½ **teaspoon baking soda**
    1 **teaspoon salt**
    1 **teaspoon caraway seeds**
    2 **eggs**
    2 **tablespoons salad oil**

1. Combine cereal and yogurt in small bowl. Let stand 5 minutes.
2. Mix flour, cheese, baking powder, soda, salt, and caraway seeds in medium-size bowl.
3. Beat eggs and oil together. Add to cereal mixture and stir.
4. Mix in flour mixture just until dry ingredients are moist.
5. Spoon into greased and floured muffin cups, filling each about ⅔ full. Bake at 375°F. for 20 to 25 minutes. Serve warm. Makes 12 muffins.

Like newborn babes, long for the pure milk of the word, that by it you may grow in respect to salvation.   1 PETER 2:2

CORNFLAKE MUFFINS

  1⅓ **cups finely crushed cornflakes**
  1⅓ **cups all-purpose flour**
    4 **teaspoons baking powder**
   ¾ **teaspoon salt**
   ⅓ **cup sugar**
    1 **egg**
  1½ **cups milk**
   ⅓ **cup vegetable oil**

1. Combine cereal, flour, baking powder, salt, and sugar.
2. Beat egg slightly in large bowl. Add milk and oil. Stir. Add cereal mixture. Mix well and let stand about 2 minutes.
3. Put batter into 12 greased 2½ inch muffin cups. Bake at 400°F. about 25 minutes, until light brown. Best served warm. Makes 12 large muffins.
Variations: Add ½ cup dates, blueberries, grated cheese, nuts, or flaked coconut to the batter before baking.

Man does not live by bread alone, but man lives by everything that proceeds out of the mouth of the LORD.   DEUTERONOMY 8:3

PRUNE MUFFINS

1¼ cups all-purpose flour
⅓ cup sugar
3½ teaspoons baking powder
1 teaspoon salt
2 cups KELLOGG'S PRODUCT 19 cereal
1¼ cups milk
1 egg
⅓ cup shortening
¾ cup coarsely chopped, pitted prunes
⅛ teaspoon cinnamon
1 tablespoon sugar

1. Combine flour, ⅓ cup sugar, baking powder, and salt in small bowl.
2. Crush cereal to 1 cup. Put in large bowl. Add milk. Stir and let stand 2 to 3 minutes, until cereal is softened.
3. Add egg and shortening, beating well.
4. Stir in prunes.
5. Add flour mixture, stirring only until dry ingredients are moistened.
6. Divide batter into 12 greased 2½ inch muffin cups. Combine cinnamon and 1 tablespoon sugar. Sprinkle over batter.
7. Bake at 400°F. about 20 minutes, until light brown. Serve warm. Makes 12 large muffins.

Give us this day our daily bread.   MATTHEW 6:11

STREUSEL COFFEE CAKE

¼ cup firmly packed brown sugar
¼ cup chopped pecans
1 tablespoon and 1 cup all-purpose flour
1 teaspoon and ⅛ teaspoon cinnamon
2 cups RICE CHEX cereal, crushed to ½ cup
¼ cup softened margarine
1 cup milk
1 beaten egg
1 teaspoon vanilla
¼ cup and 1 tablespoon sugar
1 tablespoon baking powder
½ teaspoon salt

1. Mix brown sugar, pecans, 1 tablespoon flour, and 1 teaspoon cinnamon in small bowl. Set aside.
2. Blend crushed cereal and soft margarine in large bowl. Add milk, egg, and vanilla. Beat until blended but still lumpy.
3. Sift together rest of flour, ¼ cup sugar, baking powder, and salt. Stir into liquid mixture, stirring only until dry ingredients are moist.
4. Pour half the batter into greased 8 x 8 x 2 inch pan. Sprinkle brown sugar mixture over top. Pour rest of batter into pan.
5. Bake at 400°F. for 15 minutes. Combine 1 tablespoon sugar and ⅛ teaspoon cinnamon. Sprinkle over top. Bake another 5 to 10 minutes, until pick inserted near center comes out clean. Serve warm.

BUNDT BREAKFAST RING

2 eight-ounce packages refrigerated biscuits
½ cup melted margarine
1 cup granola
¾ cup firmly packed brown sugar
1½ teaspoons cinnamon

1. After separating dough, cut each biscuit in half.
2. Dip each half in melted margarine.
3. Combine cereal, sugar, and cinnamon. Dip each buttered biscuit half in this mixture and place in greased, 12-cup Bundt pan.
4. Sprinkle rest of cereal mixture over biscuits and drizzle rest of margarine over the top.
5. Bake at 375°F. for 20 to 30 minutes. Remove from oven to serving plate. Serve warm. Makes 1 breakfast ring.

LAYERED COFFEE CAKE

2 cups all-purpose flour
½ teaspoon baking powder
½ teaspoon salt
1 cup granola
1 teaspoon cinnamon
2 tablespoons melted margarine
1 cup sour cream
1 teaspoon baking soda
½ cup softened margarine
1 cup sugar
2 eggs
½ teaspoon vanilla

1. Sift flour, baking powder, and salt together into small bowl.
2. Combine cereal, cinnamon, and the 2 tablespoons melted margarine.
3. Combine sour cream and soda.
4. Beat the ½ cup margarine and sugar together until light and fluffy. Beat eggs in, one at a time, beating well after each addition.
5. Add vanilla. Add flour mixture and sour cream alternately, adding flour mixture first and last.
6. Spread half the batter in greased 9 x 9 x 2 inch pan, then spread half the cereal mixture over the top. Repeat with rest of batter and topping.
7. Bake at 350°F. about 35 minutes, until pick inserted near center comes out clean. Cut into 9 squares.

BISCUIT COFFEE CAKE

1 package refrigerated biscuits
½ cup finely crushed cornflakes
½ teaspoon cinnamon
3 tablespoons honey
2 tablespoons melted margarine

1. Open package of refrigerated biscuits and separate them.
2. Mix cereal crumbs and cinnamon together in one bowl and honey and melted margarine in another.
3. Dip biscuits in honey mixture and then in crumb mixture.
4. Lay biscuits in greased 3-cup ring mold.
5. Bake at 400°F. about 20 minutes. Put immediately onto serving plate. Serve warm.

They might not need me,
Yet they might.
I'll let my heart
Be just in sight.
A smile as small
As mine might be
Precisely their
Necessity!
EMILY DICKINSON

CRUNCHY COFFEE CAKE

1½ **cups all-purpose flour**
2 **teaspoons baking powder**
½ **teaspoon salt**
3 **tablespoons shortening**
⅓ **cup sugar**
1 **egg**
⅔ **cup milk**
¼ **cup melted butter**
⅔ **cup sugar**
1 **teaspoon cinnamon**
¼ **teaspoon almond flavoring**
1½ **cups cornflakes**

1. Sift flour, baking powder, and salt into small bowl.
2. Cream shortening and sugar in large bowl until light and fluffy. Add egg. Beat well. Add milk. Beat well.
3. Stir flour mixture into liquid mixture, just until dry ingredients are moist.
4. Spread batter in 8 x 8 x 2 inch greased pan.
5. Combine melted butter, sugar, cinnamon, and almond flavoring. Add cereal and mix carefully until cereal is well coated.
6. Spread topping over batter. Bake at 425°F. for 25 minutes. Serve warm.

Variation: Add ½ cup flaked coconut to topping.

CINNAMON NUGGETS

MUFFINS

⅓ cup sifted all-purpose flour
1½ teaspoons baking powder
¼ teaspoon baking soda
¼ teaspoon cinnamon
5 cups RICE CHEX cereal, crushed to 1¼ cups
½ cup finely chopped pecans
⅓ cup shortening
⅔ cup firmly packed brown sugar
2 eggs
2 teaspoons vanilla
½ cup milk

TOPPING

¼ cup chopped pecans
¼ cup firmly packed brown sugar
¼ teaspoon cinnamon

1. In medium-size bowl, sift together flour, baking powder, soda, and ¼ teaspoon cinnamon.
2. Add cereal and ½ cup nuts. Mix well.
3. In large bowl, cream shortening and ⅔ cup sugar together. Beat in eggs. Add vanilla. Add cereal mixture alternately with milk.
4. Spoon batter into greased or paper-lined 2½ inch muffin cups.
5. Combine topping ingredients and sprinkle over muffins.
6. Bake at 325°F. for 30 to 35 minutes, until light brown. Makes 12 individual coffee cake nuggets.

Better is a dry morsel and quietness with it
Than a house full of feasting with strife.   PROVERBS 17:1

APRICOT BREAD

  1¾ cups all-purpose flour
   1 cup sugar
  2½ teaspoons baking powder
   1 teaspoon salt
   ¾ cup POST GRAPE-NUTS brand cereal
   ⅔ cup chopped, dried apricots
  1¼ cups milk
   1 egg, well beaten
   2 tablespoons oil

1. Combine flour, sugar, baking powder, and salt in large bowl. Add cereal and apricots. Mix well.
2. Mix milk, egg, and oil. Add flour mixture. Stir just until dry ingredients are moist.
3. Put into greased 9 x 5 x 3 inch loaf pan. Bake at 350°F. for 1 hour, until pick inserted near center comes out clean. Cool 10 minutes. Remove from pan and place on wire rack. Cool thoroughly before slicing. Makes 1 loaf.

BLUEBERRY COFFEE CAKE

  2 cups RICE CHEX cereal, crushed to 1 cup
  ¼ cup firmly packed brown sugar
  ¼ teaspoon cinnamon
  2 tablespoons melted margarine
  1 eight-ounce package refrigerated biscuits
  1 fifteen-ounce can blueberries, well-drained

1. Mix cereal, sugar, and cinnamon in large bowl.
2. Pour melted margarine over cereal mixture and stir.
3. Sprinkle half this mixture over bottom of greased 8-inch, round cake pan.
4. Arrange biscuits over cereal mixture. Arrange drained blueberries on top, then rest of cereal mixture.
5. Bake at 375°F. about 25 to 30 minutes, until pick inserted near center comes out clean. Serve warm.

Be careful of your life lest a child stumble over you.

PEANUTTY BREAD

1½ **cups all-purpose flour**
3 **teaspoons baking powder**
½ **teaspoon salt**
2 **cups raisin bran**
1⅓ **cups milk**
⅓ **cup peanut butter**
½ **cup sugar**
1 **egg**
¼ **cup chopped peanuts**

1. Sift flour, baking powder, and salt into small bowl.
2. Combine cereal and milk in small bowl. Let stand 1 or 2 minutes, until cereal softens.
3. Beat peanut butter and sugar together in large bowl. Add egg and beat well.
4. Mix in cereal mixture, then flour mixture, and then peanuts.
5. Spoon batter into greased 9 x 5 x 3 inch loaf pan. Bake at 350°F. about 1 hour, until pick inserted near center comes out clean. Cool a few minutes. Remove from pan and cool on wire rack. Makes 1 loaf.

QUICK 'N EASY BREAKFAST BUNS

2 **tablespoons margarine**
½ **cup maple-flavored syrup**
⅓ **cup granola**
10 **refrigerated packaged biscuits**

1. Melt margarine in 8-inch, round baking pan.
2. Add syrup and cereal. Mix well.
3. Arrange biscuits on top of syrupy cereal mixture.
4. Bake at 375°F. for 25 to 30 minutes. Turn upside down on serving dish and remove pan. Makes 10 sweet rolls.

APPLE BREAD

   2 cups KELLOGG'S APPLE JACKS cereal
1½ cups all-purpose flour
   2 teaspoons baking powder
  ½ teaspoon baking soda
  ¼ teaspoon salt
   1 teaspoon cinnamon
  ¼ teaspoon allspice
  ⅓ cup softened margarine
  ½ cup sugar
   2 eggs
  ½ teaspoon vanilla
  ½ cup milk
   1 cup finely chopped, pared, tart apples

1. Crush cereal to make 1 cup. Put in medium-size bowl. Add flour, baking powder, soda, salt, cinnamon, and allspice. Stir well.
2. Beat softened margarine and sugar in large bowl until well mixed. Add eggs and vanilla and beat well.
3. Add cereal mixture alternately with milk, mixing well after each addition.
4. Fold in chopped apples. Spoon batter into greased 9 x 5 x 3 inch loaf pan. Bake at 350°F. about 40 minutes, until pick inserted near center comes out clean. Cool 10 to 15 minutes before taking out of pan. Place on wire rack to continue cooling. Makes 1 loaf.

When Christ blesses the bread, it grows in our hands.

CHERRY-NUT BREAD

BREAD

  2 **cups all-purpose flour**
  3 **teaspoons baking powder**
  1 **teaspoon salt**
  ½ **teaspoon nutmeg**
  ¾ **cup sugar**
1½ **cups KELLOGG'S ALL-BRAN cereal**
1¼ **cups milk**
  1 **egg**
  2 **tablespoons vegetable oil**
  ¾ **cup chopped walnuts**
  1 **ten-ounce jar maraschino cherries,**
     drained and finely chopped

TOPPING

  1 **tablespoon margarine**
  ¼ **cup sugar**
  ¼ **cup chopped walnuts**

1. Combine flour, baking powder, salt, nutmeg, and ¾ cup sugar in medium-size bowl.
2. Mix cereal and milk in large bowl. Let stand 1 or 2 minutes, until cereal softens. Add egg and oil. Mix well.
3. Stir in flour mixture until dry ingredients are moist. Gently stir in ¾ cup walnuts and all but 2 tablespoons of the cherries. Spoon into greased 9 x 5 x 3 inch loaf pan.
4. Heat margarine in small pan until bubbly. Remove from heat and mix in ¼ cup sugar, ¼ cup walnuts, and 2 tablespoons cherries. Sprinkle over batter for a topping.
5. Bake at 350°F. about 1 hour, until pick inserted near center comes out clean. Cool about 10 minutes and remove from pan. Place on wire rack and cool completely before slicing. Makes 1 loaf.

CRANBERRY AND ORANGE BREAD

2¼ cups sifted all-purpose flour
1 cup sugar
2¼ teaspoons baking powder
1 teaspoon salt
½ teaspoon cinnamon
¼ teaspoon nutmeg
1 cup WHEAT CHEX cereal, crushed to ½ cup
⅓ cup coarsely chopped raisins
1 slightly beaten egg
2 teaspoons salad oil
½ cup orange juice
1½ tablespoons grated orange peel
1 cup drained whole cranberry sauce

1. Sift together flour, sugar, baking powder, salt, cinnamon, and nutmeg in medium-size bowl. Add cereal and chopped raisins, and stir.
2. Mix egg, oil, orange juice, grated orange peel, and drained cranberry sauce in small bowl. Stir into flour mixture, mixing just until dry ingredients are moist.
3. Pour into greased 9 x 5 x 3 inch loaf pan. Bake at 350°F. for 60 to 65 minutes, until pick inserted near center comes out clean.
4. Cool 15 minutes. Remove from pan onto cooling rack. Makes 1 loaf.

Cast your bread on the surface of the waters, for you will find it after many days.   ECCLESIASTES 11:1

BANANA-NUT LOAF

   1½ cups sifted all-purpose flour
   ½ cup sugar
   2½ teaspoons baking powder
   ½ teaspoon salt
   ½ teaspoon baking soda
   1 cup WHEAT CHEX cereal, crushed to ½ cup
   ⅓ cup chopped nuts
   1 slightly beaten egg
   ¼ cup salad oil
   2 tablespoons water
   1½ cups (3 large) mashed ripe bananas
   1 teaspoon vanilla

1. Sift together flour, sugar, baking powder, salt, and soda.
2. Add cereal and nuts. Stir.
3. Mix together egg, oil, water, bananas, and vanilla. Add to dry mixture. Mix just until dry ingredients are moist.
4. Spoon into 9 x 5 x 3 inch greased loaf pan. Bake at 350°F. for 50 to 55 minutes, until pick inserted near center comes out clean.
5. Cool about 15 minutes. Take from pan and cool on rack. Makes 1 loaf.

Before I eat,
I bow my head
And thank You, God,
For daily bread.

PINEAPPLE BREAD

2¼ cups sifted all-purpose flour
1 cup sugar
2¼ teaspoons baking powder
½ teaspoon salt
¼ teaspoon nutmeg
¼ teaspoon ginger
1½ cups RICE CHEX cereal, crushed to ¾ cup
⅓ cup chopped nuts
1 slightly beaten egg
2 tablespoons salad oil
1 eight-ounce can crushed pineapple, with liquid
¼ cup water

1. Sift together flour, sugar, baking powder, salt, nutmeg, and ginger.
2. Add cereal and nuts. Stir.
3. Mix egg, oil, pineapple with its juice, and water. Add to flour mixture, mixing just until dry ingredients are moist.
4. Pour into greased 9 x 5 x 3 inch loaf pan. Bake at 350°F. for 70 to 80 minutes, until pick inserted near center comes out clean.
5. Cool 25 minutes. Remove from pan. Cool thoroughly before slicing. Makes 1 loaf.

But you shall serve the LORD your God, and He will bless your bread and your water.   EXODUS 23:25

PUMPKIN BREAD

2½ cups sifted all-purpose flour
2½ teaspoons baking powder
1 teaspoon salt
½ teaspoon baking soda
½ teaspoon cinnamon
¼ teaspoon nutmeg
2 beaten eggs
½ cup milk
¼ cup vegetable oil
1 cup pumpkin
1¼ cups firmly packed brown sugar
1½ cups WHEAT CHEX cereal, crushed to ¾ cup
¾ cup dark raisins, coarsely chopped

1. Sift flour, baking powder, salt, soda, cinnamon, and nutmeg into medium-size bowl.
2. Mix together beaten eggs, milk, oil, pumpkin, and brown sugar.
3. Stir cereal and raisins into moist mixture. Add flour mixture and stir just until dry ingredients are moist.
4. Put in 9 x 5 x 3 inch loaf pan. Bake at 350°F. for 50 to 60 minutes, until pick inserted near center comes out clean. Cool about 15 minutes. Remove from pan and place on wire rack. Makes 1 loaf.

Variation: Raisins may be omitted.

APPLE-NUT BREAD

1¾ cups sifted all-purpose flour
2 teaspoons baking powder
¾ teaspoon salt
½ teaspoon cinnamon
¼ teaspoon nutmeg
1 cup sugar
1½ cups WHEAT CHEX cereal,
    crushed to ¾ cup
½ cup chopped walnuts
1 slightly beaten egg
3 tablespoons vegetable oil
1½ cups canned applesauce

1. Sift flour, baking powder, salt, cinnamon, nutmeg, and sugar together.
2. Stir in cereal and nuts.
3. Mix egg, oil, and applesauce. Add to dry ingredients, stirring just enough to moisten them.
4. Put in greased 9 x 5 x 3 inch loaf pan. Bake at 350°F. for 70 to 75 minutes, until pick inserted near center comes out clean.
5. Cool 15 minutes before taking out of pan. Makes 1 loaf.
Variation: Add ⅓ cup coarsely chopped raisins.

My grandfather always said that living is like licking honey off a thorn.
LOUIS ADAMIC

GRAPE-NUTS BREAD

2 cups buttermilk
1 cup POST GRAPE-NUTS brand cereal
1 cup sugar
1 slightly beaten egg
3 cups all-purpose flour
2 teaspoons baking soda
2 teaspoons baking powder
½ teaspoon salt
1 cup chopped dates or raisins
¾ cup chopped walnuts

1. Pour buttermilk over cereal. Let stand ½ hour.
2. Add sugar and egg to cereal mixture. Mix well.
3. Sift together flour, soda, baking powder, and salt. Mix into cereal mixture.
4. Blend in dates or raisins and nuts.
5. Spoon dough into greased 9 x 5 x 3 inch loaf pan and bake at 375°F. for about 45 minutes.
6. Cool a few minutes. Remove from pan and cool completely on wire rack before slicing. Makes 1 loaf.

Protect them as long as you can, while you prepare them for what's ahead.
RUTH GRAHAM

Bless, O Lord, this food to our use,
And us to Thy service,
And make us ever mindful
Of the needs of others.

BRANCAKES

1½ cups all-purpose flour
3 teaspoons baking powder
¾ teaspoon salt
2 teaspoons sugar
2 eggs
2 cups milk
1 cup KELLOGG'S BRAN BUDS cereal

1. Mix together in small bowl the flour, baking powder, salt, and sugar.
2. Beat eggs in large bowl until foamy. Add milk and cereal. Let stand 1 or 2 minutes, until cereal is softened. Stir in flour mixture, just until dry ingredients are moist.
3. Pour ¼ cup batter for each pancake on hot, greased griddle. Turning once, cook until each side is browned. Serve hot with favorite syrup. Makes 12 to 14 pancakes.

GRANOLA BREAD

2 cups all-purpose flour
¾ cup sugar
2½ teaspoons baking powder
1 teaspoon salt
1 cup granola
1 cup milk
1 beaten egg
2 tablespoons melted margarine

1. Combine flour, sugar, baking powder, and salt. Add cereal. Mix well.
2. Combine milk, beaten egg, and melted margarine. Add flour mixture and stir.
3. Spoon into greased 9 x 5 x 3 inch loaf pan. Bake at 350°F. for 45 to 55 minutes, until pick inserted near center comes out clean.
4. Cool for 10 minutes in pan. Remove and place on rack. Cool well before slicing. Makes 1 loaf.

BREAKFAST ROLLS

1½ cups BRAN CHEX cereal
¼ cup nuts
¼ cup firmly packed brown sugar
1 slightly beaten egg white
3 tablespoons light corn syrup
2 teaspoons grated orange peel
1 eight-ounce package crescent-style dinner rolls
½ cup sifted confectioners' sugar
2 teaspoons milk

1. Blend cereal and nuts in blender to make ¾ cup.
2. Put cereal mixture in large bowl. Add sugar, beaten egg white, syrup, and orange peel. Stir.
3. Divide crescent-style roll dough into 8 triangles. Spread 1½ tablespoons cereal mixture over each to within ¼ inch of edges. Roll up, from short side to point.
4. Put dough with point-side down on cookie sheet. Curve into crescents. Bake at 375°F. for 10 to 13 minutes, until light brown. Cool 10 minutes.
5. Mix confectioners' sugar and milk. Drizzle over rolls. Makes 8 breakfast rolls.

One of the most influential handclasps is that of a grandchild around the finger of a grandparent. HIGH BRIDGE, N.J., *GAZETTE*

GRANOLA PANCAKES

1 cup pancake mix
1 cup milk
1 egg
1 tablespoon liquid or melted shortening
¼ cup granola

1. Mix together pancake mix, milk, egg, and shortening, until nearly smooth.
2. Stir in cereal.
3. Pour ¼ cup batter for each pancake onto hot, greased griddle. Turn when bubbles form and edges appear cooked.
4. Serve warm with favorite syrup and more granola sprinkled on top, if desired. Makes 8 large pancakes.
   Variations: Top with fruit or mixture of honey and butter whipped together instead of syrup and cereal.

PRODUCT 19 PANCAKES

2 eggs
2 cups milk
2 tablespoons vegetable oil
4 cups KELLOGG'S PRODUCT 19 cereal, crushed
to make 1 cup
1 cup dry pancake mix

1. Beat eggs in small bowl until foamy. Add milk and oil. Stir together.
2. Combine crushed cereal and dry pancake mix in medium-size bowl. Stir in milk mixture until batter is nearly smooth.
3. Pour ¼ cup batter for each pancake on hot, greased griddle. When bubbles form, turn and cook other side. Serve warm with warm syrup. Makes 12 pancakes.

If it isn't heart-keeping, it isn't housekeeping.   MARCELENE COX

OVEN FRENCH TOAST

1 cup finely crushed cornflakes
2 eggs
¾ cup milk
½ teaspoon vanilla
8 slices day-old bread
¼ cup melted margarine

1. Put crushed cornflakes into shallow bowl.
2. In another shallow bowl, beat eggs until foamy. Mix in milk and vanilla.
3. Dip bread slices into egg mixture, turning once so both sides soak up liquid. Then dip into cereal crumbs. Put on greased cookie sheet. Drizzle melted margarine over top.
4. Bake at 450°F. about 10 minutes, until light brown. Serve warm with syrup, jelly, or honey. Serves 4 to 6.

Jesus said to them, "I am the bread of life; he who comes to Me shall not hunger, and he who believes in Me shall never thirst." JOHN 6:35

GRANOLA WAFFLES

    ¾ cup granola
    1 cup whole wheat flour
    1¾ cups all-purpose flour
    1 teaspoon salt
    1 teaspoon grated orange rind
    2 teaspoons baking powder
    2 slightly beaten eggs
    2 cups milk
    ½ cup melted margarine
    2 tablespoons honey

1. Combine cereal, whole wheat flour, all-purpose flour, salt, orange rind, and baking powder in medium-size bowl.
2. In large bowl, beat together slightly beaten eggs, milk, melted margarine, honey, and granola until smooth. Bake in heated waffle iron. Makes 5 ten-inch waffles.

Variation: Serve with orange syrup made by heating and stirring 1 cup honey, ⅓ cup orange juice, 1 tablespoon melted margarine, and ¼ teaspoon grated orange rind.

CEREAL FLAKES PANCAKES

    1 cup prepared pancake mix
    milk as directed on package
    1 cup POST GRAPE-NUTS FLAKES, crushed
    ½ cup extra milk

1. Prepare pancakes according to package directions for thin pancakes.
2. Stir in cereal and extra milk.
3. Bake on hot griddle. Serve with warm maple syrup. Makes about 12 medium-size pancakes.

Variation: Use other cereal flakes or bran cereals in place of POST GRAPE-NUTS FLAKES for variety of flavor.

2

Cakes & Pies

APPLE-SPICE CAKE

　1½　cups all-purpose flour
　2　teaspoons baking soda
　½　teaspon salt
　1　teaspoon cinnamon
　1　teaspoon nutmeg
　½　cup softened margarine
　1　cup sugar
　2　eggs
　4　cups finely chopped, peeled apples
　1　cup KELLOGG'S ALL-BRAN cereal

1. Combine in small bowl the flour, soda, salt, cinnamon, and nutmeg.

2. Beat margarine and sugar in large bowl until light and fluffy. Add eggs, beating in each one.

3. Stir in apples, cereal, and flour mixture.

4. Spoon into greased 9 x 9 x 2 inch baking pan. Bake at 350°F. about 1 hour, until cake begins to pull away from pan. Cool. Serve with ice cream, sprinkle with confectioners' sugar, or frost with favorite frosting. Serves 12.

SPECIAL K-CHOCOLATE CRUST

2 tablespoons margarine
¼ cup light corn syrup
1 six-ounce package (1 cup)
   semi-sweet chocolate chips
2 cups KELLOGG'S SPECIAL K cereal

1. In saucepan, melt and blend margarine, corn syrup, and chocolate over low heat.
2. Remove from heat and stir in cereal until well mixed.
3. Press mixture into 9-inch pie pan to form crust. Refrigerate.

SPICE CAKE

1 cup granola
1¼ cups boiling water
½ cup margarine
1¾ cups firmly packed brown sugar
1 teaspoon vanilla
2 eggs
1½ cups sifted all-purpose flour
1 teaspoon baking soda
½ teaspoon salt
¾ teaspoon cinnamon
¼ teaspoon nutmeg

FROSTING
¼ cup melted margarine
½ cup firmly packed brown sugar
3 tablespoons light cream, half and half,
   or evaporated milk
½ cup chopped nuts
¾ cup flaked coconut

1. Put cereal in small pan and stir in boiling water. Cover and allow to stand 20 minutes.
2. Beat margarine in large bowl until creamy. Add sugar slowly, beating constantly. Beat in vanilla and eggs and continue beating until fluffy.
3. Add cereal mixture and beat well.
4. Sift together flour, soda, salt, cinnamon, and nutmeg. Add to cereal mixture. Mix well.
5. Spoon batter into a greased and floured 9 x 9 x 2 inch baking pan. Bake at 350°F. for 40 to 50 minutes.
6. Combine frosting ingredients and spread on cake. Broil until bubbly. Serve warm or cool. Serves 12 to 16.

CHOCOLATE-MARSHMALLOW PIE CRUST

¾ cup miniature marshmallows
½ cup canned chocolate syrup
1 tablespoon margarine
3 cups KELLOGG'S RICE KRISPIES cereal

1. In small saucepan over low heat, mix marshmallows, chocolate syrup, and margarine. Heat until marshmallows melt, stirring to blend.
2. Put cereal in large bowl. Pour chocolate mixture over cereal until evenly coated. Save ½ cup cereal mixture for topping.
3. Press remaining cereal mixture into greased 9-inch pie plate to form crust. Freeze.
4. Fill frozen shell with any desired ice cream filling. Let set at room temperature 10 to 15 minutes before serving. Serves 6.

PINEAPPLE CAKE

3 cups RICE CHEX cereal, crushed to 1½ cups
⅓ cup firmly packed brown sugar
1 teaspoon cinnamon
2 tablespoons softened margarine
1 eight-ounce can crushed pineapple,
**   drained (save liquid)**
1 nine-ounce package yellow cake mix

1. Mix crushed cereal, sugar, and cinnamon. Reserve 1 cup of this mixture. Mix margarine with rest of cereal mixture.
2. Using pineapple juice as part of required liquid, follow package directions to prepare cake.
3. Pour half the cake batter into greased 8 x 8 x 2 inch pan. Distribute pineapple on top. Sprinkle with cup of reserved crumbs. Pour rest of batter into pan. Top with crumb and margarine mixture.
4. Bake at temperature given for cake mix 35 to 45 minutes, until pick inserted near center comes out clean. Serve fresh with whipped topping, if desired. Serves 9.

Friendly suggestions are as pleasant as perfume.
                    PROVERBS 27:9, *The Living Bible*

RICE KRISPIES CAKE

½ cup and ½ cup soft margarine
¾ cup firmly packed brown sugar
1 teaspoon almond extract
4 cups KELLOGG'S RICE KRISPIES cereal,
crushed to 2 cups
¾ cup sugar
2 eggs
2 cups sifted all-purpose flour
1½ teaspoons baking powder
¼ teaspoon salt
½ cup milk

1. Cream ½ cup margarine and brown sugar well. Add flavoring. Stir in cereal crumbs.
2. Cream other ½ cup margarine and sugar. Beat in eggs one at a time.
3. Sift together flour, baking powder, and salt. Add to egg mixture alternately with milk, beating after each addition.
4. Pour half the batter into a greased 9 x 9 x 2 inch pan. Cover with half the cereal mixture. Repeat.
5. Bake at 350°F. for 35 to 40 minutes, until pick inserted near center comes out clean. Serves 9 to 12.

Bless, Heavenly Father, this food to our use and us to Thy service, through Christ our Lord. AMEN.

BASIC CHEX CRUST

4 cups any CHEX cereal, crushed to 1 cup
¼ cup firmly packed brown sugar
⅓ cup melted margarine

1. Mix cereal crumbs with brown sugar. Stir in margarine and mix well.
2. Press into greased 9-inch pie pan to form crust. Bake at 300°F for 10 minutes. Crust will be soft.
3. Cool completely before filling.
   Variations: Add ⅓ cup chopped, salted peanuts.
   Substitute ⅓ cup flaked coconut for ⅓ cup cereal.
   Add ¼ teaspoon cinnamon.

GRANOLA BUNDT CAKE
CAKE
       ¾ cup boiling water
       1 cup granola
       1 cup margarine
       2 cups sugar
       4 eggs
       1 teaspoon vanilla
       3 cups sifted all-purpose flour
       ½ teaspoon baking soda
       ½ teaspoon salt
       ½ teaspoon nutmeg
       1 eight-ounce carton (1 cup) plain yogurt
FROSTING
       1 cup confectioners' sugar
       5 teaspoons milk
       ¼ teaspoon vanilla

1. Pour boiling water over cereal. Let set while mixing other ingredients.
2. Beat margarine and sugar until light and fluffy. Add eggs, beating after each one. Add vanilla.
3. Combine flour, salt, soda, and nutmeg. Add to creamed mixture, alternately with yogurt. Beat after each addition.
4. Stir in cereal.
5. Pour batter into greased and floured bundt pan. Bake at 325°F. about 70 minutes. Cool 10 minutes. Remove from pan and cool on rack.
6. Combine frosting ingredients and drizzle over cake.
   Variation: Also good unfrosted.

COCONUT PIE CRUST
       1½ cups POST GRAPE-NUTS FLAKES,
           slightly crushed
       ⅓ cup flaked coconut
       3 tablespoons brown sugar
       2 tablespoons chopped nuts
       3 tablespoons melted margarine

1. Stir together crushed cereal, coconut, brown sugar, and nuts. Mix in melted margarine.
2. Press into 9-inch pie pan to form crust. Bake at 350°F. for 8 to 10 minutes.
3. Cool. Fill with ice cream or any desired pie filling.

PEANUT BUTTER PIE CRUST

⅓ cup peanut butter
½ cup light corn syrup
2 cups KELLOGG'S RICE CRISPIES cereal

1. Blend peanut butter with corn syrup.
2. Stir in cereal until evenly coated.
3. Press mixture into 8-inch pie pan to form crust. Refrigerate.
4. Fill with ice cream or any other desired filling.

Do all the good you can,
By all the means you can,
In all the ways you can,
In all the places you can,
To all the people you can,
As long as you can.

JOHN WESLEY

MOCHA SNACKING CAKE

1½ cups all-purpose flour
1 teaspoon baking soda
½ teaspoon salt
1 teaspoon cinnamon
1 cup sugar
¼ cup unsweetened cocoa
½ cup KELLOGG'S BRAN BUDS cereal
1 cup cold, strong coffee
¼ cup vegetable oil
1 tablespoon vinegar
1 teaspoon vanilla

1. Combine flour, soda, salt, cinnamon, sugar, and cocoa in small bowl.
2. Put cereal and coffee into ungreased 8 x 8 x 2 inch pan. Stir. Allow to stand 1 or 2 minutes, until cereal softens. Add oil, vinegar, and vanilla. Stir. Stir in flour mixture until batter is smooth.
3. Bake at 350°F. for about 40 minutes, until pick inserted near center comes out clean. Cool in pan. Cut into 9 squares. Serve with ice cream or whipped topping. Serves 9.

Variation: Substitute 1 cup of whole wheat flour for 1 cup regular all-purpose flour.

DATE-BRAN PIE CRUST

 1 cup chopped dates
 ¼ cup water
 ⅓ cup margarine
 1½ cups KELLOGG'S ALL-BRAN cereal
 2 tablespoons sugar
 ½ cup chopped nuts

1. Cook dates and water until blended into a soft paste.
2. Stir margarine into hot mixture. Set aside.
3. Crush cereal into fine crumbs. Add sugar and nuts.
4. Combine cereal and date mixtures. Blend well. Press into 9-inch pie pan to form crust. Chill. Fill with any preferred pie filling.

A candle loses nothing by lighting another candle.

CEREAL-TOPPED CAKE

CAKE

 1¼ cups all-purpose flour
 ¾ cup sugar
 1½ teaspoons baking powder
 ½ teaspoon salt
 ¾ cup milk
 ¼ cup softened shortening
 ½ teaspoon vanilla
 1 egg

TOPPING

 ¾ cup granola
 ½ cup all-purpose flour
 ¼ cup sugar
 ½ teaspoon cinnamon
 dash of salt
 3 tablespoons melted margarine

1. Mix 1¼ cups flour, ¾ cup sugar, baking powder, and ½ teaspoon salt in a large bowl. Add milk, softened shortening, and vanilla. Beat until smooth. Add egg and beat well. Pour into greased 9-inch, round layer pan.
2. Mix cereal, ½ cup flour, ¼ cup sugar, cinnamon, and dash of salt in small bowl. Slowly add until crumbly.
3. Sprinkle top with cereal mixture. Bake at 350°F. for 45 minutes. Serve warm. Serves 6.

MARSHMALLOW CREAM CRUST

¼ **cup margarine**
1 **cup marshmallow cream**
½ **cup flaked coconut**
¼ **teaspoon vanilla**
1½ **cups crushed RICE CHEX cereal**

1. In large, heavy saucepan, heat margarine and marshmallow cream over low heat, stirring as mixture melts. Remove from heat.
2. Stir coconut, vanilla, and crushed cereal into marshmallow mixture until well mixed.
3. Press into buttered 9-inch pie pan to form crust. Chill and fill as desired.

STREUSEL CAKE

CAKE
3 **eggs**
1½ **cups firmly packed brown sugar**
1 **teaspoon vanilla**
1¾ **cups sifted all-purpose flour**
2 **teaspoons baking powder**
½ **teaspoon salt**
¾ **cup milk**
3 **tablespoons melted margarine**

FILLING
¾ **cup granola**
2 **tablespoons melted margarine**
¼ **cup firmly packed brown sugar**
½ **teaspoon cinnamon**

FROSTING
1 **cup confectioners' sugar**
5 **teaspoons milk**
¼ **teaspoon vanilla**

1. Beat eggs in large bowl until thick. Add sugar slowly, beating until light and fluffy. Add vanilla.
2. Sift flour, baking powder, and salt into egg mixture. Mix well.
3. Scald milk. Add milk and margarine to egg mixture. Pour into greased 13 x 9 x 2 inch pan.
4. Mix filling ingredients until cereal is coated. Sprinkle over batter. Bake at 350°F. about 30 to 35 minutes. Cool.
5. Combine frosting ingredients and drizzle over cake.

GRANOLA-CHOCOLATE CRUST

3 squares semi-sweet chocolate (3 ounces)
¼ cup margarine
1½ cups granola

1. In large saucepan, melt chocolate and margarine together over low heat.
2. Stir cereal into chocolate mixture to coat evenly.
3. Spoon mixture into 9-inch pie pan and form crust. Refrigerate until firm.
4. Fill with ice cream or other chilled filling.

FROZEN LEMON PIE

CRUST
2 cups cornflakes, crushed fine to ¾ cup
2 tablespoons sugar
dash of salt
¼ cup melted margarine

FILLING
2 eggs, separated
1 can (1⅓ cups) sweetened condensed milk
⅓ cup lemon juice
½ teaspoon grated lemon rind
3 tablespoons sugar

1. Stir together cereal crumbs, sugar, salt, and melted margarine. Reserve ¼ cup for topping.
2. Press remaining mixture into 9-inch pie pan to form crust. Chill before filling.
3. Beat egg yolks until thick. Add sweetened condensed milk, lemon juice, and lemon rind, stirring until well blended and thickened.
4. In separate bowl, beat egg whites until soft peaks form. Gradually add sugar and beat at high speed until stiff peaks form.
5. Fold meringue into lemon mixture until blended. Spoon into chilled crust. Top with reserved crumbs. Wrap and freeze.
6. Before serving, let stand at room temperature for 10 to 15 minutes.

Love seeks not limits but outlets.

CHERRY-CHEESE PIE
CRUST
> 3 cups KELLOGG'S RICE KRISPIES cereal,
> crushed to 1½ cups
> ¼ cup sugar
> ½ teaspoon cinnamon
> ⅓ cup melted margarine

FIRST LAYER
> 4 packages (3 ounces each)
> cream cheese, softened
> 2 eggs
> 1 teaspoon vanilla
> ⅓ cup sugar
> 1 teaspoon lemon juice

SECOND LAYER
> 1 cup (8 ounces) sour cream
> 3 tablespoons sugar

THIRD LAYER
> 1 can (1 pound 5 ounces)
> cherry pie filling
> 1 teaspoon lemon juice

1. Combine crushed cereal, ¼ cup sugar, and cinnamon in large bowl. Add melted margarine.
2. Press cereal mixture into 9-inch pie pan to form crust. Put aside.
3. For first layer, beat cream cheese until smooth. Mix in eggs, vanilla, ⅓ cup sugar, and 1 teaspoon lemon juice.
4. Pour cheese mixture into cereal crust and bake at 350°F. until set, about 25 to 30 minutes.
5. Prepare second layer by blending sour cream with 3 tablespoons sugar.
6. When pie is baked, remove from oven and spread sour cream mixture on top. Bake for 5 more minutes. Cool.
7. For third layer, mix pie filling with 1 teaspoon lemon juice and spoon on top of pie.
8. Chill before serving.

MINT-CHOCOLATE SWIRL PIE

CRUST
    ½ cup light corn syrup
    ¼ teaspoon salt
    1 six-ounce package (1 cup)
      semi-sweet chocolate chips
    2½ cups KELLOGG'S RICE KRISPIES cereal
    ½ cup chopped pecans

FILLING
    1 quart green mint ice cream
    2 tablespoons chocolate syrup

1. In large saucepan, combine corn syrup and salt. Cook over low heat until syrup simmers.
2. Stir chocolate into mixture until melted. Remove from heat.
3. Stir cereal and pecans into chocolate mixture. Spoon into 9-inch pie pan and form crust.
4. Cool crust at room temperature.
5. Pack half of ice cream into cool crust. Drizzle with chocolate syrup.
6. Repeat with remaining ice cream and syrup. Serve at once or store in freezer until ready to serve.

FROZEN CREAM PIE

CRUST
    4½ cups KELLOGG'S SUGAR FROSTED FLAKES
      cereal
    ⅓ cup melted margarine

FILLING
    1¼ cups cold milk
    1 cup heavy cream
    ½ teaspoon almond flavoring
    1 three-and-three-quarter-ounce package
      vanilla instant pudding mix

1. Crush cereal into fine crumbs. Mix with melted margarine. Set aside ⅓ cup of mixture.
2. Press remainder of buttered crumbs onto bottom and sides of 8-inch pie pan. Chill.
3. Combine milk and cream in small bowl. Stir in almond flavoring and pudding mix. Beat 1 minute to mix well.
4. Pour pudding mixture into chilled crust. Sprinkle with rest of crumb mixture. Freeze 4 hours, until firm.
5. Remove from freezer 15 minutes before serving. Serves 6.
   Variation: Substitute evaporated milk for heavy cream for a less rich filling.

PECAN-BRAN PIE

⅔ cup sugar
¼ cup melted margarine
¾ cup light corn syrup
3 beaten eggs
1 teaspoon vanilla
1½ cups BRAN CHEX cereal, crushed to ½ cup
½ cup chopped pecans
1 unbaked pie shell
6 pecan halves

1. Mix together sugar, margarine, and syrup. Blend in eggs, vanilla, cereal crumbs, and chopped pecans.
2. Fill unbaked pie crust with mixture. Garnish with pecan halves.
3. Place pie on cookie sheet and bake at 375°F. until set, about 30 to 35 minutes.
4. Cool before serving. Top with whipped topping if desired.

He that gives good advice, builds with one hand; he that gives good counsel and example, builds with both; but he that gives good admonition and bad example, builds with one hand and pulls down with the other.   FRANCIS BACON

MAPLE-HONEY-RAISIN PIE

¼ cup margarine
½ cup maple flavored syrup
½ cup honey
3 eggs
1 teaspoon vanilla
dash of salt
1 cup granola
½ cup chopped raisins
1 unbaked 8-inch pie shell

1. Cream margarine with syrup and honey until smooth.
2. Blend in eggs, vanilla, and salt.
3. Add cereal and raisins, stirring until evenly distributed.
4. Pour into unbaked pie shell. Bake at 350°F. about 50 minutes, until top is puffed and golden brown.
5. Cool pie slightly and top with ice cream, if desired.

BROWNIE PIE

½ cup POST GRAPE-NUTS brand cereal
½ cup warm water
¾ cup sugar
1 cup light corn syrup
2 squares unsweetened chocolate
3 tablespoons margarine
3 eggs
1 teaspoon vanilla
½ cup chopped pecans
1 unbaked 9-inch pie shell

1. Mix cereal and water in small bowl. Let stand until water has been absorbed.
2. Combine sugar and syrup in medium-size saucepan. Bring to a boil quickly, stirring until sugar dissolves. Boil 2 minutes. Remove from stove. Add chocolate and margarine, stirring until mixture is smooth.
3. Beat eggs slightly. Stir chocolate mixture slowly into eggs. Add soaked cereal, vanilla, and pecans.
4. Pour into favorite pie shell. Bake at 375°F. about 45 minutes, until filling is puffed across top. Serve warm or cool. Good topped with ice cream.

Pleasant words are a honeycomb,
Sweet to the soul and healing to the bones.

PROVERBS 16:24

HONEY-DATE PIE

¼ cup softened margarine
⅓ cup honey
⅔ cup light corn syrup
3 eggs
1 teaspoon vanilla
¾ cup KELLOGG'S BRAN BUDS cereal
¾ cup cut, pitted dates
1 unbaked pie shell

1. Beat softened margarine with honey and corn syrup until creamy.
2. Add eggs and blend well. Add vanilla, cereal, and dates.
3. Pour date mixture into any unbaked crust. Bake at 350°F. about 55 minutes, until set.
4. Cool pie before serving. Top with whipped topping or ice cream if desired.

LAYERED APPLE CAKE

CAKE

- ¾ cup margarine
- ¾ cup firmly packed brown sugar
- 1 egg
- ¾ teaspoon vanilla
- 1½ cups sifted all-purpose flour
- ¾ teaspoon baking powder
- ½ teaspoon salt
- ½ teaspoon cinnamon
- ⅓ cup milk
- 1½ cups WHEAT CHEX cereal, crushed to ½ cup
- 2 cups peeled apple slices
  confectioners' sugar

TOPPING

- ½ cup all-purpose flour
- ¼ cup sugar
- ¼ cup firmly packed brown sugar
- ½ teaspoon cinnamon
- ¼ cup margarine

1. Cream margarine and sugar in large bowl. Beat in egg. Add vanilla.
2. Sift together the sifted flour, baking powder, salt, and cinnamon. Add to creamed mixture. Mix well.
3. Stir in milk and cereal. Set aside.
4. Prepare topping by mixing dry ingredients in small bowl and cutting in margarine until formed into coarse crumbs.
5. Spread half the batter in greased 9-inch, round cake pan. Cover with half the apple slices, then half the topping. Repeat. Bake at 375°F. about 40 to 50 minutes, until cake begins to pull away from pan and topping is warmed. Sprinkle confectioners' sugar lightly over top. Serve warm. Serves 6 to 8.

PEACH AND PECAN CAKE

    2 cups sifted all-purpose flour
    3 teaspoons baking powder
 ½ teaspoon baking soda
 ½ teaspoon salt
 ½ cup plus 2 tablespoons margarine
    1 cup firmly packed brown sugar
    3 cups CORN CHEX cereal, crushed to 1 cup
 ⅔ cup chopped pecans
    2 beaten eggs
    1 cup milk
    1 cup whipping cream
 1½ to 2 cups sliced peaches, sweetened

1. Sift together sifted flour, baking powder, soda, and salt.
Cut in margarine and sugar to form coarse crumbs.
2. Stir in cereal and nuts.
3. Mix in beaten eggs and milk just until dry ingredients are
moist. Put in 3 greased 8-inch, round layer cake pans.
4. Bake at 350°F. for 15 to 20 minutes, until pick inserted
near center comes out clean. Cool about 15 minutes and
remove from pans.
5. When ready to serve, whip cream. Place ⅓ of peaches and
cream between each layer and on top. Makes one 3-layer
cake.

Well done is better than well said.   BENJAMIN FRANKLIN

BRAN-RAISIN SNACK CAKE

BARS
     1 cup all-purpose flour
     ½ teaspoon baking powder
     ½ teaspoon salt
     2 cups KELLOGG'S CRACKLIN' BRAN cereal
     ¾ cup milk
     ½ cup softened margarine
     1 cup firmly packed brown sugar
     2 eggs
     1 teaspoon vanilla
     ½ cup seedless raisins

GLAZE
     1 cup sifted confectioners' sugar
     1 tablespoon softened margarine
     ½ teaspoon vanilla
     2 tablespoons milk

1. Sift together flour, baking powder, and salt in small bowl.
2. In another small bowl, mix cereal and milk. Let stand 2 or 3 minutes, until cereal is softened.
3. In medium-size bowl, cream margarine and sugar until fluffy. Beat in eggs and vanilla. Stir in cereal mixture and raisins, then flour mixture. Mix well. Spread in greased 9 x 9 x 2 inch pan.
4. Bake at 350°F. about 35 minutes, until pick inserted near center comes out clean. Cool on wire rack. Cut into 16 squares.
5. For glaze, beat together confectioners' sugar, softened margarine, vanilla, and milk. Drizzle over cooled cake.

Good family life is never an accident but always an achievement by those who share it.   JAMES H. W. BOSSARD

The best gifts are tied with heartstrings.

CHOCOLATE CHIP PUMPKIN CAKE

2 cups all-purpose flour
2 teaspoons baking powder
1 teaspoon baking soda
½ teaspoon salt
1½ teaspoons cinnamon
½ teaspoon ground cloves
¼ teaspoon allspice
¼ teaspoon ginger
2 cups sugar
4 eggs
2 cups (1-pound can) pumpkin
1 cup vegetable oil
1 cup KELLOGG'S ALL-BRAN cereal
1 six-ounce package chocolate chips
1 cup coarsely chopped nuts

1. Combine flour, baking powder, soda, salt, spices, and sugar in medium-size bowl.
2. Beat eggs in large bowl until foamy. Stir in pumpkin, oil, and cereal. Add flour mixture. Stir only until combined.
3. Stir in chocolate chips and nuts.
4. Put batter in lightly greased 10 x 4 inch tube pan. Bake at 350°F. about 70 minutes, until pick inserted near center comes out clean.
5. Cool. Remove from pan. Serve plain or with whipped topping. Serves 16 to 20.
   Variations: Use KELLOGG'S Bran Buds cereal or bran flakes instead of KELLOGG'S All-Bran cereal.
   Carob chips can be substituted for chocolate chips.

A good example is worth a thousand sermons.

The teaching of the wise is a fountain of life.   PROVERBS 13:14

PEAR AND BRAN GINGER CAKE
1 **sixteen-ounce can pear halves**
1 **fourteen-and-a-half ounce package gingerbread mix**
1 **cup and ¾ cup wheat biscuits**
  water
1 **egg**
2 **tablespoons vegetable oil**
½ **cup firmly packed brown sugar**
⅔ **cup flaked coconut**
¼ **cup melted margarine**
2 **tablespoons milk**

1. Drain juice from canned pears, saving the juice. Set aside 4 pear halves. Dice the rest.
2. In large bowl, combine gingerbread mix and 1 cup cereal.
3. Measure pear syrup and add enough water to make 1¼ cups liquid.
4. Add liquid, egg, and oil to dry mixture. Beat well. Mix in diced pears.
5. Pour into greased and floured 9 x 9 x 2 inch pan. Bake at 350°F. about 35 minutes, until pick inserted near center comes out clean.
6. Split pear halves and arrange on gingerbread. Mix ¾ cup cereal, brown sugar, coconut, margarine, and milk. Spread over pears. Broil until bubbly and light brown. Top with whipped topping if desired. Serves 9.

To give children good instruction and a bad example is but beckoning to them with the head to show them the way to heaven, while we take them by the hand and lead them in the way to hell.

ARCHBISHOP TILLOTSON

The next voice you hear may be your own and it may be remembered forever by the listener. It may go down in the annals of history for someone. And it may direct that little listener toward God or away from him.   CLARISSA START

GINGER CUPCAKES
CUPCAKES
   ¼ cup margarine
   ½ cup firmly packed brown sugar
   1¼ cups sifted all-purpose flour
   ¾ teaspoon baking soda
   ½ teaspoon salt
   ½ teaspoon cinnamon
   ½ teaspoon ginger
   1 beaten egg
   ½ cup water
   ¼ cup light molasses
   1 cup WHEAT CHEX cereal, crushed to ½ cup
   ½ cup dark raisins
FROSTING
   3 ounces cream cheese
   ½ teaspoon milk
   1½ cups sifted confectioners' sugar
   1 teaspoon grated orange peel

1. Cream margarine and sugar in large bowl.
2. In small bowl, sift together flour, soda, salt, cinnamon, and ginger.
3. Stir together beaten egg, water, molasses, and crushed cereal. Add to creamed mixture alternately with flour mixture. Mix well.
4. Add raisins.
5. Spoon into greased muffin cups. Bake at 350°F. about 25 minutes.
6. Beat together cream cheese and milk until light and fluffy. Beat in confectioners' sugar. Stir in orange peel. Frost cupcakes when cool. Makes 12 frosted cupcakes.

We thank Thee for our daily bread,
Let also, Lord, our souls be fed.
O Bread of Life, from day to day
Sustain us on our homeward way.

DATE-NUT-HONEY CAKE

¾ cup sifted all-purpose flour
1 teaspoon baking powder
½ teaspoon salt
¼ cup chopped nuts
½ cup chopped dates
½ cup soft margarine
¾ cup sugar
3 eggs, separated
½ teaspoon vanilla
½ cup KELLOGG'S ALL-BRAN cereal
3 tablespoons milk

TOPPING
½ teaspoon cornstarch
1½ tablespoons honey
3 tablespoons orange juice

1. Sift flour, baking powder, and salt into small bowl. Add nuts and dates.
2. Beat margarine and sugar in large bowl.
3. Add egg yolks, vanilla, and cereal. Beat well.
4. Add flour mixture alternately with milk, beating after each addition.
5. Beat egg whites in small bowl until stiff but not dry. Fold into batter.
6. Put batter in greased and lightly floured 8 x 8 x 2 inch baking pan. Bake at 350°F. about 40 minutes.
7. Mix topping ingredients. Pour over cake while warm. Cool. Store in tightly covered container. Serves 9.

Saying is one thing, doing is another.

LEMON CAKE
CAKE
  1½ cups cornflakes
  1½ cups all-purpose flour
    1 teaspoon baking powder
   ½ teaspoon salt
   ½ cup softened margarine
  1¼ cups sugar
    2 eggs
   ½ cup milk
     grated peel of 1 lemon
   ½ cup finely chopped walnuts
SAUCE
   ½ cup sugar
    1 tablespoon cornstarch
    1 cup water
    3 tablespoons margarine
    1 teaspoon grated lemon peel
    3 tablespoons lemon juice

1. Crush cereal to make ½ cup crumbs.
2. Combine flour, baking powder, and salt.
3. Beat margarine and sugar in large bowl until light and fluffy. Beat in eggs. Stir in milk. Mix in flour mixture. Add grated lemon peel, walnuts, and cereal crumbs.
4. Put in greased 8 x 8 x 2 inch pan. Bake at 325°F. about 40 minutes, until pick inserted near center comes out clean.
5. For sauce, mix sugar, cornstarch, and water in small saucepan. Cook over medium heat until thick and clear, stirring constantly. After removing from heat, stir in margarine, lemon peel, and lemon juice. Serve warm or cool over cake. Serves 12.

3
Candies

DATE BALLS

½ cup margarine
1½ cups cut, pitted dates
⅓ cup chopped maraschino cherries
¾ cup sugar
3 cups KELLOGG'S SPECIAL K cereal
1 cup chopped nuts

1. Combine margarine, dates, maraschino cherries, and sugar in medium-size saucepan. Cook over medium heat, stirring continuously, until mixture is pasty.
2. Remove from heat. Add cereal and nuts. Stir.
3. Shape into small balls. Cool. Makes 3½ dozen.

Often one is asked, "How does one get children to have compassion and love for others?" One important way is by demonstrating love and compassion in action, not just talking about it. I do not mean organizational action but human care, in taking time, thought, energy, imagination, and creativity to fulfill some total stranger's need.

EDITH SCHAEFFER

GRANOLA TREATS

½ cup crunchy-style peanut butter
¼ cup honey
⅔ cup coconut
1 cup granola, slightly crushed

1. Stir together peanut butter, honey, coconut, and ¼ cup cereal.
2. Shape into small balls. Roll in remaining cereal.
3. Store covered in refrigerator. Makes 2 to 3 dozen. Freezes well.

PEANUT BUTTER BALLS

½ cup sugar
½ cup light corn syrup
¾ cup peanut butter
3 cups KELLOGG'S SPECIAL K cereal

1. Stir sugar and syrup together in medium-size saucepan. Bring to a boil over medium heat.
2. Remove from heat and stir in peanut butter.
3. Pour mixture over breakfast cereal and stir.
4. Form into balls. Put on waxed paper to cool. Makes about 3 dozen.

It is not enough to tell a child not to do this or that. He must be given something to do. His mind is active and his body full of energy. If a child is not given a profitable occupation, the Devil will give him something to do. He has plenty of work for idle hands.   HAROLD F. TUGGY

HONEY AND PEANUT BUTTER BALLS

1½ cups honey
2 cups peanut butter
4 cups dry powdered milk
2 cups crushed cornflakes

1. Put honey and peanut butter into medium-size bowl. Stir well.
2. Add powdered milk gradually, mixing after each addition.
3. Shape into balls. Roll each ball in crushed cornflakes. Chill. Makes about 7 dozen.
Variation: Wheat or bran flakes can be used in place of cornflakes.

RICE KRISPIES DROPS

1 pound marshmallows
1 six-ounce package (1 cup) chocolate chips
3 tablespoons margarine
½ cup chopped nuts
1½ cups KELLOGG'S RICE KRISPIES cereal
1 teaspoon vanilla

1. Melt marshmallows, chocolate chips, and margarine over low heat or over hot water in double boiler.
2. After removing from heat, add nuts, cereal, and vanilla. Mix well.
3. Drop by tablespoonfuls onto greased cookie sheet. Chill. Makes about 30 candies.

Of course, when it comes right down to it, the best way to impart faith to a child is to live faith in front of him. A child can see right through phonies. They pick up what our relationship with God and Christ really is.
ARVELLA SCHULLER

CHOCOLATE MOUNDS

2 six-ounce packages chocolate chips
4 cups wheat flakes

1. Melt chocolate chips in double boiler over hot water.
2. When chocolate has cooled to room temperature, stir in cereal until well coated.
3. Drop by tablespoonfuls onto cookie sheet. Chill at least 2 hours.
   Variations: Add ¼ cup toasted almonds.
   Toasted oat cereal or cornflakes can be used in place of wheat flakes.
   Butterscotch chips can be used in place of chocolate chips.

PEANUT BUTTER DROPS

½ cup light or dark corn syrup
½ cup sugar
1 cup peanut butter
2 cups cornflakes

1. Heat corn syrup and sugar together until sugar dissolves.
2. Add peanut butter. Stir until well blended.
3. Add cornflakes. Drop mixture by teaspoonfuls onto waxed paper.
4. Remove when cool.

Thank you, God,
For milk and bread
And other things so good;
Thank you, God,
For those who help
To grow and cook our food.
ELIZABETH McE. SHIELDS

BUTTERSCOTCH CLUSTERS

1 cup butterscotch chips
1 tablespoon peanut butter
2 cups KELLOGG'S RICE KRISPIES cereal

1. Combine butterscotch chips and peanut butter in medium-size saucepan. Melt and stir together over medium heat.
2. Remove from heat. Stir in cereal until well coated.
3. Drop by tablespoonfuls onto cookie sheet or waxed paper.
4. Chill until firm.

PEANUT BUTTERSCOTCH DROPS

1 six-ounce package (1 cup) butterscotch chips
¼ cup peanut butter
3 cups KELLOGG'S PRODUCT 19 cereal

1. Combine butterscotch chips and peanut butter in medium-size saucepan. Melt over low heat, stirring continuously.
2. After removing from heat, add cereal. Stir well.
3. Drop by tablespoonfuls onto greased cookie sheet. Press mixture firmly to desired shape. Chill. Makes about 24 candies.

While we place the helping hand on a child's, wouldn't this be an excellent opportunity to teach him the lesson of a lifetime: that he needs God's hand on his? How much frustration he will be spared through learning early that God's strength is made perfect (and demonstrated to other people) as we allow Him to help us in our weakness.

JEANETTE LOCKERBIE

FUDGE DROPS

1 six-ounce package (1 cup) chocolate chips
1 six-ounce package (1 cup) butterscotch chips
1¼ cups granola
1 cup coarsely chopped peanuts

1. Melt chocolate and butterscotch chips in top of double boiler over hot, but not boiling, water.
2. Stir in cereal and peanuts.
3. Drop by teaspoonfuls onto cookie sheet lined with waxed paper.
4. Store in refrigerator.

CHOCOLATE CRISPS

1 six-ounce package (1 cup) chocolate chips
1½ cups KELLOGG'S RICE KRISPIES cereal
½ cup raisins

1. Melt chocolate chips in double boiler.
2. Add cereal and raisins. Mix well.
3. Drop by tablespoonfuls on waxed paper.
4. Cool. Makes about 18.

Children require spiritual food as well as a balanced diet for physical growth. You are concerned about giving them the proper amounts of proteins, fats, and carbohydrates. You should be equally conscientious about feeding them the pure Word of God. Children need multiple vitamins to grow strong in body. They also must have spiritual vitamins so that "the inner man may be renewed day by day" (2 Corinthians 4:16).
ELSIE D. HOLSINGER

DATE 'N CHOCOLATE DROPS

1 pound sweet milk chocolate
2 one-ounce squares unsweetened chocolate
1 cup chopped pecans
1 cup chopped dates
¼ teaspoon salt
5 cups cornflakes

1. Combine two chocolates in top of double boiler. Melt over hot water.
2. Mix nuts, dates, salt, and cereal. Stir into melted chocolate.
3. Drop by teaspoonfuls onto waxed paper. Chill at least 1 hour. Makes about 5 dozen.

FRUIT AND BRAN TREAT

> 2½ cups KELLOGG'S ALL-BRAN cereal
> 1 cup chopped dates
> ¾ cup light raisins
> ¾ cup shredded coconut
> ¾ cup chopped, toasted almonds
> 1½ teaspoons grated lemon peel
> 1 fourteen-ounce can sweetened condensed milk
> 2 tablespoons lemon juice

1. Mix cereal, dates, raisins, coconut, almonds, and lemon peel in large bowl.
2. Mix sweetened condensed milk and lemon juice in small bowl. Add to cereal mixture. Mix well.
3. Drop by teaspoonfuls onto cookie sheet. Chill in refrigerator. Makes about 4 dozen.

Some children are never given the thrill of putting forth effort and receiving the rewards of that effort — not only material reward but the deep satisfaction of accomplishment.   ELLEN McKAY TRIMMER

SWEET GRAHAM CLUSTERS

> ½ pound white candy coating
> 3 cups GOLDEN GRAHAMS breakfast cereal
> ½ cup salted peanuts
> ½ cup miniature marshmallows

1. Cut white candy coating into small pieces. Put in 10 inch, heavy skillet. Cover and heat over low heat about 5 minutes, until soft. Remove from heat. Stir until creamy.
2. Fold in cereal until coated. Carefully stir in peanuts and marshmallows.
3. Drop by tablespoonfuls onto waxed paper. Chill until firm. Makes about 2 dozen.

CHOCOLATE-PEANUT CRUNCHIES

1 six-ounce package chocolate chips
1 tablespoon peanut oil
½ cup smooth peanut butter
2 tablespoons confectioners' sugar
about 80 bite-size wheat biscuits
about 40 peanuts

1. Melt and blend together chocolate chips and peanut oil in top of double boiler over hot water.
2. Blend in peanut butter and sugar. Cool slightly.
3. Coat each small biscuit with mixture. Place on waxed paper.
4. Press half a peanut into top of each. Chill. Makes 6 to 7 dozen.

A child is like a delicate camellia whose petals are marred by thoughtless handling. ELSIE D. HOLSINGER

ALMOND BARK CANDY

2 cups KELLOGG'S RICE KRISPIES cereal
½ cup salted peanuts
1 pound almond bark candy

1. Put cereal and peanuts in large bowl.
2. Melt almond bark candy in double boiler over gently boiling water.
3. Pour melted candy over cereal and peanuts, stirring until well coated.
4. Spread on waxed paper or greased cookie sheet. Cool in refrigerator about 15 minutes or more.
5. Break into pieces. Makes 2 to 3 dozen.
   Variations: Use KELLOGG'S FROOT LOOPS cereal in place of KELLOGG'S RICE KRISPIES cereal.
   Substitute chopped pecans for peanuts.
   Add 1 cup miniature marshmallows.
   Add 2 tablespoons peanut butter to basic recipe.

CHEX PEANUT BRITTLE

1 cup firmly packed brown sugar
¼ cup light corn syrup
½ cup water
1 teaspoon salt
¾ cup cocktail peanuts
¼ teaspoon baking soda
2 tablespoons margarine
5 cups CORN CHEX cereal

1. Combine sugar, corn syrup, water, and salt in large, heavy saucepan. Cook to hard ball stage (250°F.) over medium heat.
2. Stir in nuts. Cook and stir over low heat until a little mixture dropped in cold water becomes brittle (285°F.). Remove from heat.
3. Blend in soda and margarine. Stir in cereal until well coated. Spread quickly on greased cookie sheet.
4. Use 2 greased forks to separate into thin layer. When cool, break into small pieces. Makes about 1 pound.

The way you teach is very important, and what you teach is even more important, but how you live is most important.

CARAMEL CANDY

1 fourteen-ounce package caramels
(about 48 caramels)
¼ cup milk
½ cup peanut butter
5 cups RICE CHEX cereal, crushed to 2½ cups

1. Combine caramels and milk in top of double boiler. Melt and stir over hot water until smooth. Remove from heat.
2. Blend in peanut butter.
3. Put cereal in large greased bowl. Pour caramel mixture over cereal, and mix until coated.
4. Press into greased 8 x 8 x 2 inch baking pan with greased spoon.
5. Cool. Cut into small squares. Store loosely covered. Makes about 5 dozen.

CAROL'S CORNFLAKE CANDY

½ cup corn syrup
½ cup firmly packed brown sugar
¾ cup peanut butter
¼ cup margarine
1 teaspoon vanilla
6 cups cornflakes
   pinch of salt

1. Combine corn syrup and brown sugar over low heat.
2. When well blended, add peanut butter, margarine, and vanilla. Mix well and remove from heat.
3. Stir in cereal and salt.
4. Press into greased 8 x 8 x 2 inch pan. Cut into 16 squares.
Variation: Substitute KELLOGG'S Rice Krispies cereal for cornflakes.

What we value as grandmothers is the child. What is a clean kitchen worth, compared with the joy of a child who has actually produced a miniature loaf of bread with his or her own hands?

RUTH GOODE

QUICK FUDGE

¼ cup margarine
1 six-ounce package (1 cup) chocolate chips
¼ cup corn syrup
1 teaspoon vanilla
1½ cups sifted confectioners' sugar
2 cups KELLOGG'S RICE KRISPIES cereal

1. Combine margarine, chocolate chips, corn syrup, and vanilla in large saucepan. Cook and stir over low heat until smooth. Remove from heat.
2. Add sugar, mixing well. Stir in cereal until well coated.
3. Press into greased 8 x 8 x 2 inch pan. Chill until firm. Cut into 25 squares.

PUDDING SQUARES

4 cups sugar frosted flakes
½ cup chopped pecans
1 four-and-a-half-ounce package chocolate instant pudding mix
½ cup light corn syrup

1. Put 2½ cups cereal in large bowl. Add nuts and stir.
2. Crush rest of cereal slightly and put in small bowl.
3. Blend pudding mix into corn syrup. Pour over cereal and nut mixture and mix together.
4. Press into greased 8 x 8 x 2 inch baking dish. Sprinkle crushed cereal over top, and press in. Chill until firm. Cut into squares.
Variation: Substitute butterscotch instant pudding for chocolate.

Dear Lord, thou giver of all good,
Rest Thy hand upon this food;
Bless it, that our lives may be
A constant service unto Thee.

CHOCOLATE CEREAL CANDY

⅓ cup light corn syrup
½ cup firmly packed brown sugar
½ cup crunchy-style peanut butter
3 cups KELLOGG'S COCOA KRISPIES cereal

1. Combine corn syrup and brown sugar in large saucepan.
2. Cook over medium heat, stirring often, until bubbles form around edges. Remove from heat.
3. Stir in peanut butter until well blended.
4. Add cereal and stir until well coated.
5. Press into greased 8 x 8 x 2 inch pan.
6. Cool at room temperature. Cut into 24 squares.

S'MORE BARS

⅓ **cup light corn syrup**
1 **tablespoon margarine**
1 **six-ounce package (1 cup) chocolate chips**
½ **teaspoon vanilla**
4 **cups GOLDEN GRAHAMS breakfast cereal**
1½ **cups miniature marshmallows**

1. In large saucepan, combine corn syrup and margarine. Bring to boil over medium heat. Remove from heat.
2. Stir in chocolate chips and vanilla until chocolate melts.
3. Gradually add cereal, mixing gently until well coated. Stir in marshmallows.
4. Press into greased 9 x 9 x 2 inch pan with greased spoon. Cool at room temperature. Cut into 24 bars.

The wise in heart will be called discerning,
And sweetness of speech increases persuasiveness.   PROVERBS 16:21

FUDGE SANDWICHES

1 **six-ounce package (1 cup) butterscotch chips**
½ **cup crunchy-style peanut butter**
4 **cups KELLOGG'S RICE KRISPIES cereal**
1 **six-ounce package (1 cup) chocolate chips**
½ **cup sifted confectioners' sugar**
2 **tablespoons margarine**
1 **tablespoon water**

1. Combine butterscotch chips and peanut butter in large saucepan. Melt and stir until smooth. Remove from heat.
2. Stir in cereal until well coated.
3. Press half cereal mixture into greased 8 x 8 x 2 inch pan. Chill.
4. Combine chocolate chips, confectioners' sugar, margarine, and water in top of double boiler over hot water. Heat and stir until smooth. Spread over top of chilled cereal mixture.
5. Distribute rest of cereal mixture over top. Press down. Chill at least 1 hour. Cut into 25 squares.

PUFFED WHEAT CANDY

⅓ cup margarine
1 cup firmly packed brown sugar
½ cup light corn syrup
2 tablespoons cocoa
1 teaspoon vanilla
8 cups puffed wheat

1. Combine margarine, brown sugar, corn syrup, and cocoa in medium-size saucepan.
2. Over medium heat, bring to rolling boil. Boil 1 minute. Remove from heat. Stir in vanilla.
3. Put cereal in large, greased bowl or pan.
4. Pour syrup mixture over cereal. Mix well.
5. Press onto greased cookie sheet with buttered spoon.
6. Chill in refrigerator. Cut into squares. Makes 70 squares.

I love these little people; and it is not a slight thing, when they, who are so fresh from God, love us.   CHARLES DICKENS

CHOCOLATE-PEANUT BUTTER TREATS

¼ cup margarine
1 cup confectioners' sugar
¼ teaspoon vanilla
½ cup chocolate chips
1 cup crunchy-style peanut butter
¾ cup KELLOGG'S RICE KRISPIES cereal

1. Cream together margarine and sugar.
2. Melt chocolate over hot water in double boiler.
3. Add peanut butter, melted chocolate, and vanilla to creamed mixture. Blend well to form stiff dough.
4. Roll dough between sheets of waxed paper to thickness of ¼ inch.
5. Sprinkle half the cereal on dough and fold over, keeping cereal on inside.
6. Roll out to thickness of about ½ inch.
7. Sprinkle rest of cereal over dough. Again fold over and roll out to about ½ inch thickness.
8. Cut into small pieces. Chill. Makes about 3 dozen.

POPCORN CANDY

3 cups popped corn
1 cup nuts
1 cup shredded coconut
3 cups cornflakes
1 cup sugar
1 cup light corn syrup
½ cup cream

1. Mix popped corn, nuts, coconut, and cereal and place in a greased 9 x 12 inch baking dish.
2. Cook sugar, syrup, and cream until a spoonful dropped in cold water forms a soft ball.
3. Pour syrup over popped corn mixture, mix well, cool, and cut into squares. Makes about 20 squares.

We all have had occasion to observe our own behavior mirrored in the actions of our children, sometimes as they have played with their dolls and toys, sometimes in their attitudes towards their playmates.

JEANETTE LOCKERBIE

RICE AND PEANUT BUTTER LOGS

1 cup peanut butter
1 cup and ½ cup confectioners' sugar
2 tablespoons softened margarine
1½ cups KELLOGG'S RICE KRISPIES cereal
1½ tablespoons milk
½ cup flaked coconut

1. Combine peanut butter, 1 cup confectioners' sugar, and softened margarine in large bowl. Chill.
2. Shape into logs.
3. Mix together ½ cup confectioners' sugar and milk. Roll logs in this mixture, then in coconut. Makes 4 or 5 logs. Refrigerate. Slice each log into about 12 pieces.

DATE-NUT LOGS

½ cup melted margarine
1 cup sugar
1 cup chopped dates
½ cup chopped nuts
1 beaten egg
1 teaspoon vanilla
2½ cups puffed rice
½ cup coconut
½ cup chopped nuts

1. In medium-size saucepan, combine melted margarine, sugar, chopped dates, ½ cup chopped nuts, and beaten egg.
2. Cook together over low heat for 10 minutes. Remove from heat. Add vanilla.
3. Put cereal in large bowl. Pour hot mixture over cereal. Let cool about 30 minutes. Shape into 2- to 3-inch logs. Combine coconut and ½ cup chopped nuts. Roll logs in this mixture and place on cookie sheet. Chill in refrigerator. Makes 24 logs.

DAVE'S PEANUT-CHOCOLATE SWIRLS

    ¾ cup sugar
    ¾ cup corn syrup
    ¾ cup peanut butter
   4½ cups KELLOGG'S RICE KRISPIES cereal
    1 twelve-ounce package (2 cups)
       chocolate chips, melted
    ½ cup chopped peanuts

1. Combine sugar and corn syrup in large saucepan. Over medium heat, cook and stir constantly until mixture bubbles. Remove from heat.
2. Add peanut butter and stir until well blended. Add cereal. Stir until cereal is coated.
3. Press mixture while still warm into greased 11 x 16 inch jelly roll pan.
4. Spread melted chocolate over cereal mixture. Sprinkle chopped peanuts over chocolate. Cut mixture in half crosswise.
5. Roll each half to form 2 logs. Wrap each in waxed paper. Chill in refrigerator until firm. Remove from refrigerator. After 15 minutes, cut into half-inch slices. Makes 40 slices.

Cookies

CHOCOLATE SWIRLS

1¾ cups all-purpose flour
½ teaspoon baking soda
½ teaspoon salt
1 cup softened margarine
1 cup sugar
2 eggs
1 teaspoon vanilla
3 cups sugar frosted flakes,
   crushed to measure 1½ cups
1 six-ounce package (1 cup)
   chocolate chips, melted

1. Sift flour, soda, and salt together in small bowl.
2. In large bowl, cream margarine and sugar until fluffy. Beat in eggs and vanilla.
3. Add flour mixture to creamed mixture. Mix well.
4. Stir in crushed cereal.
5. Drizzle melted chocolate over dough. Swirl through dough for marbled look.
6. Drop by rounded tablespoonfuls onto ungreased cookie sheets.
7. Bake at 350°F. for 10 to 13 minutes, until light brown. Place immediately on wire racks. Makes about 5 dozen cookies.

For each cup and plateful,
Make us truly grateful.

CHOCOLATE CHIP FAVORITES

2¼ cups all-purpose flour
1 teaspoon baking soda
½ teaspoon salt
1 cup softened margarine
¾ cup sugar
¾ cup firmly packed brown sugar
2 eggs
1 teaspoon vanilla
2 cups KELLOGG'S RICE KRISPIES cereal
1 six-ounce package (1 cup)
    chocolate chips

1. Combine flour, soda, and salt in small bowl.
2. In large bowl, cream margarine and sugars together. Beat in eggs and vanilla.
3. Add flour mixture to creamed mixture. Mix well.
4. Stir in cereal and chocolate chips.
5. Drop by tablespoonfuls onto greased cookie sheets.
6. Bake at 350°F. about 10 minutes, until light brown. Cool briefly and place on wire racks. Makes about 5 dozen cookies.
Variations: Add ¾ cup peanut butter to creamed mixture.
Substitute KELLOGG'S All-Bran or Bran Buds cereals for KELLOGG'S Rice Krispies cereal.

You can preach a better sermon with your life than with your lips.
                                          OLIVER GOLDSMITH

KRINKLY BUTTERSCOTCH DROPS

2¾ cups sifted all-purpose flour
1 teaspoon baking soda
1 teaspoon salt
2 teaspoons vanilla
1½ cups margarine
3 cups firmly packed brown sugar
4 unbeaten eggs
1 twelve-ounce package cornflakes (8 cups)

1. Sift together the sifted flour, soda, and salt.
2. Add vanilla to margarine. Cream together, gradually adding sugar. Cream until light and fluffy.
3. Add eggs to creamed mixture, one at a time, beating well. Add flour mixture and beat.
4. Fold in cereal. Drop by teaspoonfuls onto greased cookie sheets.
5. Bake at 350°F. about 10 minutes, until crisp and light brown. Makes 7 dozen.

PEANUT BUTTER FAVORITES

½ cup margarine
1 cup sugar
1 egg
1 teaspoon vanilla
½ cup crunchy-style peanut butter
1¼ cups all-purpose flour
1 teaspoon baking soda
½ teaspoon salt
2 tablespoons milk
1½ cups POST GRAPE-NUTS FLAKES

1. In large bowl, cream margarine and sugar together. Beat in egg and vanilla. Blend in peanut butter.
2. Sift together flour, soda, and salt. Add to creamed mixture alternately with milk.
3. Stir in cereal.
4. Drop by teaspoonfuls onto ungreased cookie sheets.
5. Bake at 350°F. for 10 to 12 minutes. Cool slightly and place on wire racks. Makes about 4 dozen cookies.
   Variation: Any cereal flakes may be substituted for POST GRAPE-NUTS FLAKES.

EASY PEANUT BUTTER DROPS

½ cup sugar
½ cup light corn syrup
dash of salt
1 cup crunchy-style peanut butter
3 cups KELLOGG'S RICE KRISPIES cereal

1. Combine sugar, corn syrup, and salt in medium-size saucepan. Bring to boil.
2. After removing from heat, add peanut butter. Beat well. Stir in cereal.
3. Drop by teaspoonfuls onto waxed paper. Makes about 4 dozen cookies.

Blessed are children who have parents and grandparents who can relate the stories of their own pasts and so connect the younger with older memories, lighting a taper in the imagination that never goes out.
                                                    GRACE E. KING

PEANUT BUTTER COOKIES

⅓ cup soft shortening
⅔ cup peanut butter
1 cup firmly packed brown sugar
2 eggs
2 cups sifted all-purpose flour
½ teaspoon salt
½ teaspoon baking soda
¼ cup milk
1 cup crushed CAP'N CRUNCH

1. Beat together in large bowl shortening, peanut butter, and brown sugar until creamy.
2. Add eggs. Beat well.
3. Sift flour, salt, and soda into small bowl. Add alternately with milk to creamed mixture.
4. Stir in crushed cereal.
5. Drop by teaspoonfuls onto ungreased cookie sheets. Press with fork tines to make crisscross marks on each. Bake at 350°F. for 10 to 12 minutes. Makes 3 to 4 dozen cookies.

MACAROONS

2 egg whites
⅛ teaspoon salt
1 cup sugar
1 cup shredded coconut
2 cups coarsely crushed cornflakes
½ teaspoon almond flavoring

1. Beat egg whites and salt until stiff.
2. Add sugar. Beat well.
3. Fold in coconut and cereal.
4. Stir in flavoring.
5. Drop by teaspoonfuls onto greased cookie sheets. Bake at 325°F. about 15 minutes, until light brown. Makes about 2½ dozen cookies.

With honest intent and a genuine desire to see our children live for God, let's pray for wisdom to make our own faith so attractive to them that they will taste and come back for more.

JEANETTE LOCKERBIE

COCONUT CHEWS

1 cup shortening
1 cup sugar
1 cup firmly packed brown sugar
2 eggs
2 cups all-purpose flour
1 teaspoon baking soda
½ teaspoon baking powder
2 cups flaked coconut
2 cups WHEATIES breakfast cereal
1 teaspoon vanilla

1. Cream shortening and sugars together in large bowl. Add eggs and beat well.
2. Sift together flour, soda, and baking powder. Add to creamed mixture.
3. Stir in coconut, cereal, and vanilla.
4. Drop by teaspoonfuls onto greased cookie sheets. Bake at 375°F. for 10 to 15 minutes. Makes about 7 dozen cookies.

Once truth is firmly planted in a child, it continues steadfast through any test, but the planting has to be done early in the growing season.
MARCELENE COX

COCONUT DROP COOKIES

½ cup margarine
1 cup sugar
2 eggs, separated
2 tablespoons milk
2 cups sifted all-purpose flour
1 teaspoon salt
1 teaspoon baking powder
1 cup chopped raisins
1 cup shredded coconut
2 teaspoons vanilla
3 cups whole cornflakes

1. Cream margarine and sugar in large bowl.
2. Beat egg yolks in small bowl. Combine with milk. Add to creamed mixture.
3. Sift together flour, salt, and baking powder. Add to first mixture.
4. Stir in raisins and coconut.
5. In small bowl, beat egg whites until stiff. Fold egg whites into other mixture. Add vanilla and cereal. Stir carefully.
6. Drop by teaspoonfuls onto greased cookie sheets. Bake at 300°F. about 20 minutes, until lightly browned. Makes 3 to 4 dozen cookies.

A gentle answer turns away wrath.   PROVERBS: 15:1

FRUIT-FLAVORED COOKIES

COOKIES
2 cups all-purpose flour
½ teaspoon baking powder
¼ teaspoon salt
1 cup softened margarine or
  other shortening
½ cup sugar
2 eggs
½ cup orange juice
2 cups KELLOGG'S FROOT LOOPS cereal,
  crushed to fine crumbs

ICING
2 cups sifted confectioners' sugar
3 tablespoons softened margarine
2 tablespoons orange juice

1. Combine flour, baking powder, and salt in small bowl.
2. In large bowl, cream together margarine or other shortening with sugar until fluffy. Beat in eggs and juice.
3. Add flour mixture to creamed mixture. Mix well. Stir in crushed cereal. Drop by tablespoonfuls onto ungreased cookie sheets.
4. Bake at 350°F. about 12 minutes. Remove from cookie sheets at once and place on wire racks to cool.
5. Beat together confectioners' sugar, 3 tablespoons margarine, and 2 tablespoons orange juice. Spread over tops of cooled cookies. Sprinkle crushed cereal over tops, if desired. Makes about 4 dozen cookies.

One thing we need never be afraid of is having our child mimic us in being kind and loving to others, beginning in our own home.
JEANETTE LOCKERBIE

Make home happy, and you will be happy at home.

ICED SANDWICH COOKIES

WAFERS

1½ cups all-purpose flour
¾ teaspoon salt
½ cup softened margarine
1 cup sugar
1 egg
1 teaspoon vanilla
2 one-ounce squares
   unsweetened chocolate, melted
2 cups KELLOGG'S RICE KRISPIES cereal,
   crushed to measure 1 cup
¾ cup coarsely chopped nuts

ICING

1½ cups sifted confectioners' sugar
2 tablespoons softened margarine
4 teaspoons milk
1 teaspoon vanilla
¼ cup finely chopped nuts

1. Combine flour and salt in small bowl.
2. In large bowl, cream margarine and sugar. Beat in egg, vanilla, and melted chocolate.
3. Add flour mixture to creamed mixture. Mix well.
4. Stir in crushed cereal and chopped nuts.
5. Drop by rounded teaspoonfuls onto lightly greased cookie sheets. Press dough into flat circles.
6. Bake at 325°F. about 10 minutes. Cool slightly and place on wire racks to finish cooling.
7. For icing, beat together confectioners' sugar, softened margarine, milk, and vanilla in small bowl.
8. Spread icing on half the cookies. Top each with unfrosted cooky. Ice tops and sprinkle with ¼ cup finely chopped nuts. Makes about 3 dozen sandwich cookies.

ORANGE GUMDROP COOKIES

1 cup shortening
1 cup sugar
1 cup firmly packed brown sugar
3 eggs
1 teaspoon vanilla
2 cups all-purpose flour
1 teaspoon baking powder
1 teaspoon baking soda
½ teaspoon salt
1 cup oatmeal
1 cup bran flakes
1 cup coconut
1 cup nuts
1 cup orange gumdrop slices
   cut into small pieces

1. Cream shortening and sugars. Beat in eggs. Add vanilla.
2. Sift together flour, baking powder, soda, and salt. Add to first mixture.
3. Stir in oatmeal, cereal, coconut, nuts, and candy.
4. Drop by teaspoonfuls onto greased cookie sheets. Bake at 375°F. for 12 to 15 minutes. Makes 4 to 5 dozen cookies.

Great God, we praise Thy gracious care,
Thou dost our daily bread prepare;
O bless the earthly food we take,
And feed our souls, for Jesus' sake.

COCONUT-OATMEAL COOKIES

½ cup margarine or other shortening
½ cup sugar
½ cup firmly packed brown sugar
1 egg
½ teaspoon vanilla
1 cup all-purpose flour
½ teaspoon baking soda
¼ teaspoon baking powder
¼ teaspoon salt
1 cup oatmeal
1 cup WHEATIES breakfast cereal
½ cup shredded coconut

1. Cream together shortening and sugars. Add egg and mix well. Add vanilla.
2. Combine flour, soda, baking powder, and salt. Add to creamed mixture. Stir in oats, cereal, and coconut.
3. Drop by rounded teaspoonfuls onto ungreased cookie sheets. Bake 8 to 12 minutes at 375°F. Makes 3 to 4 dozen cookies.

Variation: Add 1 six-ounce (1 cup) package chocolate, butterscotch, or peanut butter chips.

RANCH COOKIES

1 cup all-purpose flour
¼ teaspoon baking powder
½ teaspoon baking soda
½ teaspoon salt
⅔ cup margarine
1 cup firmly packed brown sugar
1 well-beaten egg
1 teaspoon vanilla
¾ cup oatmeal
½ cup chopped nuts
1 cup chopped dates
1 cup cornflakes

1. In small bowl, sift together flour, baking powder, soda, and salt.
2. Cream margarine and sugar together in large bowl. Add beaten egg and vanilla. Mix well.
3. Add flour mixture to creamed mixture. Mix well.
4. Add oats, nuts, and dates, and stir.
5. Carefully stir in cereal.
6. Drop by teaspoonfuls onto ungreased cookie sheets. Bake at 350°F. about 10 to 12 minutes. Makes 3 dozen cookies.

NUT DROP COOKIES

½ cup shortening
1 cup firmly packed brown sugar
2 eggs
1 teaspoon vanilla
1¼ cups all-purpose flour
1 teaspoon baking powder
½ teaspoon salt
1 cup coarsely chopped nuts
4 cups WHEATIES breakfast cereal

1. Combine shortening, brown sugar, eggs, and vanilla in large bowl, mixing well.
2. Sift flour to measure. Add baking powder and salt to flour, and mix.
3. Add flour mixture to shortening mixture.
4. Stir in nuts. Fold in cereal.
5. Drop by teaspoonfuls onto greased cookie sheets. Bake at 375°F. for 8 to 10 minutes. Makes 4 to 5 dozen cookies.

The availability of grandparents and their homes could be said to double a child's opportunities to form favorable attitudes.

BETTY LAND

CHEWY WALNUT COOKIES

1½ cups all-purpose flour
½ teaspoon baking soda
1 teaspoon salt
1 cup softened margarine
1 cup sugar
½ cup firmly packed brown sugar
1 egg
1 teaspoon vanilla
1 cup chopped walnuts
2 cups KELLOGG'S PRODUCT 19 cereal,
crushed to measure 1 cup

1. Combine flour, soda, and salt in small bowl.
2. In large bowl, beat margarine and sugars together until light and fluffy.
3. Beat in egg and vanilla.
4. Add flour mixture and mix well.
5. Stir in walnuts and crushed cereal.
6. Drop by teaspoonfuls onto ungreased cookie sheets. Bake at 350°F. for 13 to 15 minutes, until golden brown. Cool slightly and place on wire racks to finish cooling. Makes 4 to 5 dozen cookies.

We thank Thee, loving Father,
For all Thy tender care,
For food and clothes and shelter,
And all Thy world so fair. AMEN.

CORNFLAKE ROCKS

  ½ cup butter
  ½ cup sugar
  ½ cup firmly packed brown sugar
  1 egg
  1 cup sifted all-purpose flour
1½ teaspoons baking powder
  ¼ teaspoon salt
  1 cup shredded coconut, toasted
  1 cup cornflakes

1. Cream butter and sugars together in medium-size bowl.
2. Beat in egg.
3. Sift together flour, baking powder, and salt. Blend into creamed mixture.
4. Stir in toasted coconut and cereal.
5. Drop by tablespoonfuls onto ungreased cookie sheets. Bake at 350°F. for 10 minutes. Cool slightly. Remove from cookie sheets. Makes 2 to 3 dozen cookies.

GOLDEN GRAHAM COOKIES

½ cup margarine
⅓ cup sugar
⅓ cup firmly packed brown sugar
1 egg
½ teaspoon vanilla
1 cup all-purpose flour
½ teaspoon baking soda
¼ teaspoon baking powder
¼ teaspoon salt
½ cup shredded coconut
2 cups GOLDEN GRAHAMS breakfast cereal

1. Cream margarine and sugars together in large bowl. Add egg and vanilla. Mix well.
2. Sift together flour, soda, baking powder, and salt. Blend into creamed mixture.
3. Gently stir in coconut and cereal.
4. Drop by rounded teaspoonfuls onto ungreased cookie sheets.
5. Bake at 350°F. for 10 to 12 minutes. Cool a few minutes and place on wire racks. Makes 3 to 4 dozen cookies.

CHOCO-PEANUT BUTTER COOKIES

½ cup margarine
½ cup creamy peanut butter
½ cup sugar
½ cup firmly packed brown sugar
2 eggs
1 teaspoon vanilla
1 cup sifted all-purpose flour
1 teaspoon baking soda
¼ teaspoon salt
1½ cups BRAN CHEX cereal,
   crushed to ½ cup
1 six-ounce package (1 cup)
   chocolate chips

1. In large bowl, cream margarine, peanut butter, and sugars until fluffy. Beat in eggs and vanilla.
2. In small bowl, sift together flour, soda, and salt. Blend into creamed mixture.
3. Stir in cereal crumbs and chocolate chips.
4. Drop by tablespoonfuls onto greased cookie sheets.
5. Bake at 350°F. for 7 to 9 minutes. Cool briefly and place on wire racks. Makes about 5 dozen cookies.

The greatest thing a man can do for his heavenly Father is to be kind to some of His other children. HENRY DRUMMOND

CHOCO-BUTTERSCOTCH COOKIES

1½ cups all-purpose flour
½ teaspoon baking soda
½ teaspoon salt
1 cup softened margarine
1 cup sugar
½ cup firmly packed brown sugar
1 egg
1 teaspoon vanilla
2 cups KELLOGG'S COCOA KRISPIES cereal
1 six-ounce package (1 cup)
   butterscotch chips

1. Combine flour, soda, and salt in small bowl.
2. In large bowl, cream together margarine and sugars until fluffy.
3. Beat egg and vanilla into creamed mixture.
4. Blend in flour mixture.
5. Stir in cereal and butterscotch chips.
6. Drop by tablespoonfuls onto ungreased cookie sheets.
7. Bake at 350°F. about 13 to 15 minutes, until golden brown. Cool slightly and place on wire racks to finish cooling. Makes about 5 dozen cookies.

The pots and kettles in the household have the same holiness, when used in His service, as the incense bowls before the altar.

DORIS COFFIN ALDRICH

GRANOLA COOKIES

½ cup margarine
1 cup firmly packed brown sugar
1 egg
3 tablespoons milk
1 teaspoon vanilla
1½ cups all-purpose flour
½ teaspoon baking soda
¼ teaspoon salt
2 cups granola

1. Beat together margarine and brown sugar.
2. Beat in egg, milk, and vanilla.
3. Sift together flour, soda, and salt. Add to creamed mixture. Blend well.
4. Stir in granola.
5. Drop by rounded teaspoonfuls onto greased cookie sheets. Bake at 350°F. for 10 to 12 minutes. Cool on rack. Makes about 3 dozen cookies.
   Variation: Add 1 cup chocolate chips or ½ cup shredded coconut.

NUT COOKIES

1 cup all-purpose flour
½ teaspoon baking powder
½ teaspoon salt
½ teaspoon baking soda
⅓ cup margarine
½ cup sugar
½ cup firmly packed brown sugar
1 egg
1 teaspoon vanilla
1 cup POST GRAPE-NUTS FLAKES
¾ cup chopped nuts

1. In small bowl, combine flour, baking powder, salt, and soda.
2. Cream margarine and sugars together in large bowl. Beat in egg and vanilla.
3. Blend flour mixture into creamed mixture. Stir in cereal and nuts.
4. Drop by teaspoonfuls onto ungreased cookie sheets.
5. Bake at 375°F. for 10 to 12 minutes. Cool slightly and place on wire racks. Makes about 2 to 3 dozen cookies.

HERMITS

COOKIES

1¼ cups all-purpose flour
½ teaspoon baking soda
½ teaspoon cinnamon
¼ teaspoon nutmeg
¼ teaspoon ginger
2 cups bran flakes
½ cup milk
½ cup softened margarine
1 cup firmly packed brown sugar
2 eggs
1 teaspoon vanilla
½ cup coarsely chopped peanuts
1 cup seedless raisins

ICING

1½ cups sifted confectioners' sugar
2 tablespoons softened margarine
5 teaspoons milk
1 teaspoon vanilla

1. In small bowl, sift together flour, soda, cinnamon, nutmeg, and ginger.
2. In another small bowl, combine cereal and milk. Stir. Let stand 1 or 2 minutes, until cereal softens.
3. In large bowl, cream margarine and sugar together until fluffy. Beat in eggs and vanilla. Mix in cereal.
4. Blend in flour mixture. Stir in peanuts and raisins. Drop by tablespoonfuls onto lightly greased cookie sheets.
5. Bake at 375°F. for 10 to 12 minutes. Place immediately on wire racks.
6. Beat together confectioners' sugar, margarine, milk, and vanilla for icing. Frost cookies when cool. Makes about 4 dozen cookies.

He saith unto him, Feed my lambs.   JOHN 21:15, (KJV)

PECAN DROP COOKIES

        2 eggs
        1 cup sugar
        1 cup firmly packed brown sugar
       ½ cup salad oil
        1 teaspoon vanilla
       2¼ cups cornflakes
       2¼ cups oatmeal
       2¼ cups all-purpose flour
        1 teaspoon baking soda
        1 teaspoon baking powder
       ½ teaspoon salt
       ½ cup chopped pecans

1. In medium-size bowl, beat eggs until thick. Add sugars and beat. Add salad oil. Beat. Add vanilla.
2. Crush cereal. In large bowl, combine cereal, oatmeal, flour, baking soda, baking powder, salt, and nuts.
3. Stir egg mixture into dry mixture.
4. Drop by teaspoonfuls onto greased cookie sheets.
5. Bake at 350°F. for 8 to 10 minutes. Makes about 6 dozen cookies.

CINNAMON COOKIES

        1 cup softened margarine
           or other shortening
       1½ cups sugar
        2 eggs
       2¼ cups sifted all-purpose flour
        1 teaspoon baking soda
       ¼ teaspoon salt
        2 cups BRAN CHEX cereal,
           crushed to ¾ cup
        2 teaspoons cinnamon mixed
           with 3 tablespoons sugar

1. In large bowl, cream margarine or other shortening with sugar. Beat in eggs.
2. Sift together in small bowl flour, soda, and salt. Blend into creamed mixture. Stir in cereal crumbs.
3. Shape into small balls. Roll in cinnamon-sugar mixture. Place on ungreased cookie sheets.
4. Bake at 400°F. for 6 to 8 minutes. Cool briefly and place on wire racks. Makes 6 to 7 dozen cookies.

COCONUT COOKIES

1 cup margarine
1 cup sugar
1 cup firmly packed brown sugar
2 eggs
2 cups all-purpose flour
1 teaspoon baking soda
½ teaspoon baking powder
½ teaspoon salt
½ teaspoon vanilla
2 cups coconut
2 cups WHEATIES breakfast cereal

1. Cream margarine and sugars.
2. Beat in eggs.
3. Sift flour, soda, salt, and baking powder into creamed mixture. Beat well.
4. Stir in vanilla, coconut, and cereal.
5. Roll into balls, place on cookie sheets and press flat. Bake at 375°F. for about 12 minutes. Makes 4 to 5 dozen cookies.

DATE-BRAN COOKIES

½ cup softened margarine
½ cup sugar
½ cup firmly packed brown sugar
1 egg
1 tablespoon milk
1 teaspoon vanilla
1 cup sifted all-purpose flour
1 teaspoon baking powder
¼ teaspoon salt
1 cup finely chopped dates
½ cup flaked coconut
1½ cups BRAN CHEX cereal,
crushed to ½ cup

1. In large bowl, cream margarine and sugars until fluffy. Beat in egg, milk, and vanilla.
2. In small bowl, sift together flour, baking powder, and salt. Blend into creamed mixture.
3. Gently stir in dates, coconut, and cereal crumbs.
4. Drop by rounded teaspoonfuls onto greased cookie sheets.
5. Bake at 350°F. for 10 to 12 minutes. Cool briefly and place on wire racks. Makes 3 to 4 dozen cookies.

OATMEAL-NUT COOKIES

1 cup margarine
1 cup sugar
1 cup firmly packed brown sugar
2 eggs
1 teaspoon vanilla
2 cups all-purpose flour
1 teaspoon salt
1 teaspoon baking soda
2 cups oatmeal
2 cups KELLOGG'S RICE KRISPIES cereal
1 cup chopped nuts

1. Cream margarine and sugars in large bowl. Beat in eggs and vanilla.
2. Combine flour, salt, and soda. Add to creamed mixture.
3. Stir in oatmeal, cereal, and nuts.
4. Shape into round balls. Place on greased cookie sheets. Flatten with bottom of glass or tines of fork.
5. Bake at 350°F. for 12 to 15 minutes. Makes 6 to 7 dozen cookies.

For food and health and happy days,
Accept our gratitude and praise;
In serving others, Lord, may we
Repay our debt of love to Thee.

CRUNCHY COOKIE CIRCLES

1 cup all-purpose flour
2 tablespoons cornstarch
½ cup confectioners' sugar
1 cup softened margarine
1¾ cups granola

1. Combine flour, cornstarch, and sugar in medium-size bowl. Mix in margarine. Cover and chill until dough can be handled easily.
2. Shape into small balls. Roll in cereal. Place on ungreased cookie sheets. Flatten with floured fork.
3. Bake at 300°F. for 20 to 25 minutes, until light brown. Makes 3 dozen cookies.

CORNFLAKE CRUNCHIES

1½ cups dark brown sugar
2 tablespoons honey
3 tablespoons butter
1 cup milk
8 cups cornflakes

1. Stir together in medium-size saucepan brown sugar, honey, butter, and milk. Cook over low heat, stirring frequently, until mixture forms soft ball in cold water.
2. Place cereal in large, shallow pan in oven preheated to 325°F. Brown about 10 minutes.
3. Lightly butter inside of large mixing bowl. Put browned cereal in bowl. Pour hot syrup over cereal and stir with fork.
4. Shape mixture into small mounds on buttered cookie sheets. Cool and remove from sheets. Makes about 3 dozen cookies.

A child tends to accept your ideas, your philosophy, because he accepts you. And he tends to reject your ideas and philosophy when he rejects you.   HOWARD G. HENDRICKS

RICE KRISPIES COOKIES

¾ cup margarine
1 cup sugar
1 cup firmly packed brown sugar
2 beaten eggs
2 cups all-purpose flour
½ teaspoon baking powder
1 teaspoon baking soda
1 cup coconut
1 teaspoon vanilla
3 cups KELLOGG'S RICE KRISPIES cereal

1. Cream margarine and sugars together in large bowl. Beat in eggs.
2. Combine flour, baking powder, and soda. Add to creamed mixture. Mix well.
3. Stir in coconut, vanilla, and cereal.
4. Shape into small balls. Place on greased cookie sheets.
5. Bake at 350°F. for 8 to 10 minutes. Makes 6 to 7 dozen cookies.

GRANOLA-SUGAR COOKIES

3¼ cups all-purpose flour
2½ teaspoons baking powder
¾ teaspoon salt
1 cup margarine
1⅓ cups sugar
2 eggs
3 teaspoons vanilla
2 cups granola
granulated sugar

1. Combine flour, baking powder, and salt.
2. Cream margarine and sugar in large bowl, beating until light and fluffy. Add eggs one at a time, beating after each addition. Add vanilla and mix.
3. Add flour mixture a little at a time to creamed mixture, mixing well after each addition.
4. Add cereal and stir. Roll dough into small balls and place on greased cookie sheets. Press cookies flat with buttered and sugared flat-bottom glass.
5. Bake at 375°F. for 10 to 12 minutes, until edges are light brown. Makes 4 to 5 dozen cookies.

A joyful heart is good medicine.   PROVERBS 17:22

PEANUT BUTTER DELIGHTS

  1 cup softened margarine
1½ cups firmly packed brown sugar
  2 eggs
  1 cup creamy peanut butter
  2 cups sifted all-purpose flour
  2 teaspoons baking soda
 ½ teaspoon salt
  1 cup granola

1. Beat margarine and sugar in large bowl until creamy. Beat in eggs and peanut butter.
2. Sift flour, soda, and salt together. Mix into creamed mixture.
3. Stir in cereal. Chill dough for easier handling. Roll into 1-inch balls.
4. Place on ungreased cookie sheets. Press with floured fork to form criss-cross pattern.
5. Bake at 350°F. for 8 to 10 minutes. Makes about 6 dozen cookies.

Thou art great and Thou art good,
And we thank Thee for this food.
By Thy hand must all be fed;
Give us, Lord, our daily bread. AMEN.

CEREAL-COATED COOKIES

1 cup margarine
⅔ cup crunchy-style peanut butter
1 cup firmly packed brown sugar
1 egg
1 teaspoon vanilla
1½ cups all-purpose flour
½ teaspoon baking soda
¼ teaspoon salt
½ cup crushed wheat flakes

1. In large bowl, blend margarine, peanut butter, and sugar. Beat in egg and vanilla.
2. Combine flour, soda, and salt in small bowl. Add to margarine mixture. Mix well. Chill dough several hours, until firm.
3. Shape into small balls. Roll in crushed cereal. Place on greased cookie sheets.
4. Bake at 350°F. for 10 to 13 minutes. Makes about 4 dozen cookies.

PEANUTTY CRISPS

1 cup softened margarine
½ cup peanut butter
½ cup sugar
½ cup firmly packed brown sugar
1 egg
1 teaspoon vanilla
1⅓ cups sifted all-purpose flour
4 cups cornflakes, crushed
   to make 1 cup crumbs
   whole peanuts

1. Blend margarine and peanut butter in medium-size bowl. Mix in sugars. Beat in egg and vanilla.
2. Stir in flour. Mix well.
3. Shape into small balls. Roll in cereal crumbs. Place on greased cookie sheets.
4. Press one peanut into top of each ball of dough.
5. Bake at 350°F. about 15 minutes. Makes 4 to 5 dozen cookies.

God is great
And God is good;
Let us thank Him
For our food.

PEANUT-OATMEAL COOKIES

1 cup sugar
1 cup firmly packed brown sugar
1 cup shortening
2 eggs
2¼ cups all-purpose flour
1 teaspoon baking powder
1 teaspoon baking soda
1 cup salted peanuts
1 cup crushed cornflakes
1 cup oatmeal
1 teaspoon vanilla

1. In large bowl, cream sugars and shortening until light and fluffy.
2. Add eggs and beat well.
3. Sift flour, baking powder, and soda into creamed mixture. Mix well.
4. Stir in peanuts, crushed cereal, oatmeal, and vanilla.
5. Shape into small balls. Roll in granulated sugar. Place on greased baking sheets. Bake at 375°F. about 10 minutes. Makes about 5 dozen cookies.

COCONUT-BUTTERSCOTCH BARS

⅓ cup butter or other shortening
½ cup POST GRAPE-NUTS brand cereal
¾ cup firmly packed light brown sugar
1 egg
1 teaspoon vanilla
¾ cup sifted all-purpose flour
½ teaspoon baking powder
⅛ teaspoon baking soda
¼ teaspoon salt
¾ cup shredded coconut

1. Melt butter in medium-size saucepan. Add cereal and heat about 2 minutes, until cereal is soft. Remove from heat.
2. Stir in sugar. Cool a little.
3. Beat egg until thick. Add egg and vanilla to cereal mixture.
4. Sift flour and measure. Add baking powder, soda, and salt. Sift these together into small bowl.
5. Put cereal mixture in large bowl. Add flour mixture to cereal mixture gradually, stirring well. Stir in coconut.
6. Press evenly into greased 8 x 8 x 2 inch baking pan. Bake at 350°F. for 20 to 25 minutes. Cool. Cut into 15 to 20 bars.

GRANOLA-RAISIN BARS

3 cups granola, coarsely crushed
½ cup raisins
⅓ cup wheat germ
⅓ cup firmly packed brown sugar
¼ cup margarine
3 tablespoons honey

1. Mix cereal, raisins, and wheat germ in large bowl.
2. Mix sugar, margarine, and honey in small saucepan. Cook over low heat, stirring now and then, until smooth.
3. Pour warm mixture over cereal mixture. Stir well.
4. Press firmly into well-greased 8 x 8 x 2 inch pan. Bake at 350°F. for 12 to 14 minutes. Cool well. Cut into 24 bars. Store in cool place.
Variation: Substitute ⅔ cup chopped nuts or peanuts for ⅓ cup wheat germ.

ORANGE-GLAZED GRANOLA BARS

BARS
2 eggs
⅔ cup firmly packed brown sugar
¼ cup softened margarine
⅓ cup all-purpose flour
¼ teaspoon salt
⅛ teaspoon nutmeg
2 cups granola
2 tablespoons raisins
½ cup chopped walnuts
2 teaspoons grated orange rind

GLAZE
2 teaspoons margarine
2 tablespoons orange juice
¾ cup confectioners' sugar
¼ teaspoon grated orange rind

1. Beat eggs until thick. Gradually add sugar while beating. Beat in ¼ cup margarine.
2. Blend in flour, salt, and nutmeg.
3. Stir in cereal, raisins, nuts, and 2 teaspoons orange rind.
4. Spoon into greased 9 x 9 x 2 inch pan. Bake at 375°F. about 25 to 30 minutes.
5. While bars are cooking, heat 2 teaspoons margarine and 2 tablespoons orange juice together. When melted, pour over confectioners' sugar and ¼ teaspoon grated orange rind in small bowl. Beat well. Spread over warm bars.
6. Cool. Cut into 24 bars.

There is no loving others without living for others.

HENRIETTA C. MEARS

CORNFLAKE BARS

   ¼ cup margarine
   ½ cup firmly packed brown sugar
   1 cup sifted all-purpose flour
   2 eggs
   1 cup firmly packed brown sugar
   1 teaspoon vanilla
   ¼ teaspoon salt
   1 cup coconut
   1 cup chopped nuts
   1 cup cornflakes

1. Cream margarine and ½ cup brown sugar in medium-size bowl.
2. Blend in flour with fork or pastry blender.
3. Press into bottom of 13 x 9 x 2 inch pan.
4. Bake at 350°F. about 12 minutes.
5. Beat eggs well in small bowl. Add 1 cup brown sugar slowly. Add vanilla and salt. Beat well.
6. Carefully stir in coconut, chopped nuts, and cereal. Spread over baked mixture. Bake another 25 minutes. Cool slightly and cut into 20 or 24 bars.

DREAM BARS

   ⅓ cup margarine
   1½ cups crushed vanilla wafers
   1⅓ cups flaked coconut
   1 cup chocolate chips
   1 cup granola
   1 fourteen-ounce can sweetened
      condensed milk

1. Put margarine in 13 x 9 x 2 inch pan. Put in warm oven until margarine melts.
2. Spread vanilla wafer crumb over margarine and press down with fork.
3. Sprinkle coconut over the top, then chocolate chips, and then cereal.
4. Drizzle sweetened condensed milk over rest of ingredients.
5. Bake at 350°F. for 25 to 30 minutes, until light brown. Cool in pan. Cut into 24 bars.

Your influence is negative or positive, never neutral.
                                                    HENRIETTA C. MEARS

FILLED BROWNIES

BROWNIES
    2 **squares unsweetened chocolate**
    ⅓ **cup margarine**
    ⅔ **cup all-purpose flour**
    ½ **teaspoon baking powder**
    ¼ **teaspoon salt**
    1 **whole egg**
    1 **egg yolk**
    2 **tablespoons water**
    1 **cup sugar**
    1 **teaspoon vanilla**

FILLING
    1 **egg white**
    ⅓ **cup granola**
    2 **tablespoons all-purpose flour**

1. Melt chocolate and margarine in small, heavy saucepan over low heat.
2. Sift together the ⅔ cup flour, baking powder, and salt.
3. Beat together the whole egg, egg yolk, and water. Add sugar and vanilla. Beat well. Blend in chocolate and flour mixtures.
4. Pour half the batter into greased 8 x 8 x 2 inch pan.
5. Beat egg white until stiff. Add cereal and 2 tablespoons flour, stirring carefully. Spread on top of batter in pan. Top with rest of batter.
6. Bake at 350°F. for 25 minutes. Allow to cool in pan. Makes 16 squares.

BROWNIE BARS

3 cups granola
½ cup firmly packed brown sugar
½ cup margarine, melted
⅓ cup all-purpose flour
1 package brownie mix

1. Combine cereal, sugar, margarine, and flour, mixing well.
2. Spread over bottom of ungreased 13 x 9 x 2 inch pan.
3. Bake at 350°F. for 10 minutes. Cool. Follow package directions for fudge-style brownies to prepare brownie batter. Spread over baked cereal layer.
4. Bake at 350°F. about 35 minutes. Cool. Cut into 32 bars.

Lord Jesus, be our holy Guest,
Our morning joy, our evening Rest;
And with our daily bread impart
Thy love and peace to every heart. AMEN.

BRAN BROWNIES

¾ cup all-purpose flour
¼ teaspoon baking soda
¼ teaspoon salt
½ cup sugar
⅓ cup vegetable oil
2 tablespoons water
1 six-ounce package (1 cup) semi-sweet chocolate chips
1 teaspoon vanilla
2 eggs
½ cup KELLOGG'S BRAN BUDS cereal
¾ cup coarsely chopped nuts

1. Combine flour, soda, and salt in small bowl.
2. Stir sugar, oil, and water together in large saucepan. Bring to boil, stirring often. Remove from heat. Stir in chocolate chips until melted. Add vanilla. Add eggs and beat well.
3. Add flour mixture to rest and mix well. Stir in cereal and nuts. Spread dough in greased 8 x 8 x 2 inch pan.
4. Bake at 325°F. for 30 minutes, until pick inserted near center comes out clean. Cool. Cut into 16 squares.

If you want to get across an idea, wrap it up in a person.
RALPH BUNCHE

NUT BARS

BARS
1 cup sifted all-purpose flour
¾ cup sugar
½ teaspoon baking powder
¼ teaspoon salt
2 cups BRAN CHEX cereal,
crushed to ¾ cup
½ cup margarine

TOPPING
1 slightly beaten egg
¾ cup firmly packed brown sugar
½ teaspoon cinnamon
1 teaspoon vanilla
¼ cup melted margarine
¾ cup chopped nuts

1. Sift together flour, sugar, baking powder, and salt.
2. Stir in cereal crumbs.
3. Cut in margarine with 2 knives or a pastry blender until dough looks like coarse crumbs.
4. Press into bottom of greased 9 x 9 x 2 inch pan.
5. Bake at 350°F. about 12 minutes.
6. While bottom layer is cooking, mix together slightly beaten egg, brown sugar, cinnamon, and vanilla. Blend in melted margarine and chopped nuts. Spoon over bars as soon as removed from oven.
7. Return to oven and bake another 20 to 25 minutes. Cool. Cut into 20 bars.

RAISIN COOKIES

½ cup softened margarine
½ cup sugar
½ cup firmly packed brown sugar
1 egg
1 teaspoon vanilla
1 cup sifted all-purpose flour
1 teaspoon baking powder
¼ teaspoon salt
1 cup raisins
½ cup flaked coconut
3 cups RICE CHEX cereal,
  crushed to 1½ cups

1. Cream margarine and sugars together in large bowl. Beat in egg and vanilla.
2. Sift together flour, baking powder, and salt. Blend into creamed mixture.
3. Carefully stir in raisins, coconut, and cereal.
4. Drop by heaping tablespoonfuls onto cookie sheets. Flatten to about ¼-inch thick.
5. Bake at 350°F. for 10 to 12 minutes. Cool briefly and place on wire racks. Makes 3 dozen cookies.

OAT'N MARSHMALLOW BARS

32 large marshmallows
¼ cup margarine
1 teaspoon vanilla
4 cups CAP'N CRUNCH

1. Melt marshmallows and margarine in heavy saucepan over low heat or in top of double boiler over hot water.
2. After removing from heat, add vanilla.
3. Put cereal in large, greased bowl. Pour hot mixture over cereal. Stir well. Press with greased spoon into greased 9 x 9 x 2 inch pan. When cool, cut into bars. Makes 18.

If we have not thought about flour and eggs — or dress materials and knitting yarns — as educational materials when we were mothers, as grandmothers we can surely afford to.

RUTH GOODE

BUTTERSCOTCH-NUT BARS

1 pound marshmallows
3 tablespoons margarine
1¼ cups butterscotch chips
1 cup KELLOGG'S RICE KRISPIES cereal
1 cup coarsely chopped walnuts
1 teaspoon vanilla
½ teaspoon salt

1. Melt marshmallows, margarine, and butterscotch chips in heavy saucepan over low heat or in top of double boiler over hot water. Stir to blend.
2. Remove from heat.
3. Add cereal, nuts, vanilla, and salt. Press into 8 x 8 x 2 inch greased pan. Cut into 36 squares.

QUICK BUTTERSCOTCH SQUARES

1 six-ounce package (1 cup)
butterscotch chips
½ cup peanut butter
3 cups KELLOGG'S RICE KRISPIES cereal

1. Combine butterscotch chips and peanut butter in large saucepan. Stir over low heat until melted and smooth. Remove from heat.
2. Stir in cereal until well coated.
3. Press into greased 9 x 9 x 2 inch pan. Chill. Cut into 36 squares.
   Variations: With the cereal, add 1 cup salted peanuts, 1 cup raisins, or 1 cup flaked coconut.

A Chinese proverb says, "A child is like a white piece of paper on which every passerby writes a little." This tells us how important our actions, our attitudes, our ordinary day-to-day living is, and how powerfully this relational teaching affects all members of the family.

OSCAR E. FEUCHT

CHEWY GRAHAM BARS

    32 large marshmallows or 3 cups
       miniature marshmallows
    ½ cup creamy peanut butter
    ¼ cup margarine
    5 cups GOLDEN GRAHAMS breakfast cereal

1. Melt marshmallows, peanut butter, and margarine in large saucepan over low heat, stirring constantly.
2. After removing from heat, gradually stir in cereal.
3. Press firmly into 9 x 9 x 2 inch greased pan. Cool. Cut into 18 or 24 bars.

CHOCOLATE CHIP SQUARES

    ⅓ cup margarine
    ½ pound regular or miniature
       marshmallows
    5 cups KELLOGG'S SPECIAL K cereal
    ½ cup chocolate chips
    ½ cup chopped nuts

1. Melt margarine in large saucepan over low heat.
2. Add marshmallows. Heat, stirring constantly, until marshmallows melt and mixture is smooth. Remove from heat.
3. Stir in cereal until well coated.
4. Stir in chocolate chips and nuts.
5. Press into greased 13 x 9 x 2 inch pan. Cool. Cut into 24 squares.

As we go onward with God we are to teach His way to our children and to trust that they too will follow in our footsteps. The best inducement to them to a godly walk is to see that we have entered into Canaan's land or milk and honey.

V. RAYMOND EDMAN

QUICK COCOA BARS

1 **six-ounce package (1 cup) chocolate chips**
⅓ **cup peanut butter**
4 **cups KELLOGG'S COCOA KRISPIES cereal**

1. In large saucepan over low heat, melt together, stirring constantly, chocolate chips and peanut butter. When melted and well mixed, remove from heat.
2. Add cereal. Stir until coated.
3. Press into greased 9 x 9 x 2 inch pan. Chill in refrigerator. Cut into 36 bars.

ICED CHOCOLATE SQUARES

COOKIES

2 **cups granola**
3 **cups graham cracker crumbs**
1 **cup sifted confectioners' sugar**
3 **tablespoons margarine**
9 **tablespoons cocoa**
1 **cup plus 2 tablespoons evaporated milk**
1 **teaspoon vanilla**

GLAZE

1 **tablespoon margarine**
3 **tablespoons cocoa**
¾ **cup unsifted confectioners' sugar**
dash of salt
2 **tablespoons milk**

1. In large bowl, mix cereal, cracker crumbs, and confectioners' sugar.
2. Melt margarine over low heat. Add cocoa and evaporated milk. Stir until well blended. Remove from heat. Stir in vanilla.
3. Pour chocolate mixture over cereal mixture. Mix well.
4. Press into greased 9 x 9 x 2 inch pan.
5. For glaze, melt margarine over low heat. Remove from heat. Mix in confectioners' sugar and salt. Add milk, a little at a time, until right consistency to spread.
6. Spread warm icing over cookie mixture. Chill. Cut into 36 squares.

The training of children is a profession in which we must know how to lose time in order to gain it.

JEAN JACQUES ROUSSEAU

FROSTED FAVORITES

1 **cup sugar**
1 **cup light corn syrup**
1 **cup peanut butter**
6 **cups KELLOGG'S RICE KRISPIES cereal**
1 **six-ounce package (1 cup)**
  chocolate chips

1. Combine sugar and corn syrup in large saucepan. Cook over medium heat, stirring constantly, until mixture begins to boil. Remove from heat.
2. Add peanut butter. Mix well.
3. Add cereal. Stir until well coated.
4. Press into greased 9 x 13 x 2 inch pan.
5. Melt chocolate chips in double boiler over hot water. Spread over top of cookies.
6. Cool. Cut into about 24 bars.

PEANUT BARS

½ **cup light corn syrup**
¼ **cup firmly packed brown sugar**
¼ **teaspoon salt**
1 **cup peanut butter**
1 **teaspoon vanilla**
2 **cups KELLOGG'S RICE KRISPIES cereal**
1 **cup cornflakes, slightly crushed**
1 **six-ounce package (1 cup)**
  chocolate chips

1. Mix corn syrup, sugar, and salt in medium-size saucepan. Bring to boil.
2. Add peanut butter. Stir until blended.
3. After removing from heat, add vanilla, cereals, and chocolate chips. Mix well.
4. Press into greased 9 x 9 x 2 inch pan. Chill well. Cut into 18 or 24 bars.

The serene, silent beauty of a holy life is the most powerful influence in the world, next to the might of God.   BLAISE PASCAL

SPECIAL K FROSTED BARS

    ⅔   **cup light corn syrup**
    ⅔   **cup sugar**
    ¾   **cup crunchy-style peanut butter**
    1   **teaspoon vanilla**
    4½   **cups KELLOGG'S SPECIAL K cereal**
    1   **six-ounce package (1 cup)**
      butterscotch chips
    ½   **six-ounce package (½ cup)**
      chocolate chips

1. Combine corn syrup and sugar in medium-size saucepan. Bring to slow boil. Remove from heat.

2. Blend peanut butter into hot syrup mixture. Stir in vanilla.

3. Put cereal in large bowl. Pour warm mixture over cereal and stir until cereal is coated. Press into lightly greased 13 x 9 x 2 inch pan.

4. Melt butterscotch and chocolate chips in double boiler over hot, but not boiling, water. Spread over cereal mixture.

5. When cool, cut into bars or squares. Makes about 2½ or 3 dozen.

CHOCOLATE-BANANA BARS

BARS

    1 cup all-purpose flour
    ½ teaspoon baking powder
    ¼ teaspoon baking soda
    1 teaspoon salt
    ½ teaspoon cinnamon
    ¼ cup softened margarine
    ¾ cup sugar
    1 cup mashed, fully ripe bananas
      (about 3 medium-size)
    1 egg
    ¼ cup milk
    1 cup KELLOGG'S ALL-BRAN cereal
    1 six-ounce package (1 cup)
      chocolate chips, melted
    1 cup chopped nuts

FROSTING

    2 tablespoons margarine
    1 six-ounce package (1 cup)
      semi-sweet chocolate chips
    1 cup sifted confectioners' sugar
    ¼ cup milk
    ⅛ teaspoon salt
    ¼ teaspoon vanilla

1. Combine flour, baking powder, soda, salt, and cinnamon in small bowl.
2. In large bowl, beat together margarine, sugar, mashed bananas, egg, milk, cereal, and melted chocolate.
3. Add flour mixture to creamed mixture and mix well.
4. Stir in nuts.
5. Put batter in greased and floured 13 x 9 x 2 inch pan.
6. Bake at 350°F. about 30 minutes, until pick inserted near center comes out clean. Cool in pan.
7. Make frosting by melting margarine and chocolate chips together and then stirring in confectioners' sugar, milk, salt, and vanilla.
8. Spread on frosting. Cut into 32 bars.

SUGAR-SPRINKLED BROWNIE SQUARES

6 cups cornflakes, crushed
  to make 2¾ cups
1 cup chopped walnuts
½ cup confectioners' sugar
1 teaspoon grated orange peel
1 six-ounce package (1 cup)
  chocolate chips
1 cup evaporated milk

1. Put finely crushed cereal into large bowl.
2. Add nuts, sugar, and orange peel. Stir.
3. Heat chocolate chips and milk together at low heat in heavy saucepan, stirring constantly.
4. When chocolate has melted and mixture is smooth, stir in cereal mixture until blended.
5. Press into greased 9 x 9 x 2 inch pan. Chill about 45 minutes until almost firm. Cut into 25 or 36 squares. Chill completely.
6. Sprinkle tops with confectioners' sugar before serving.

For food and drink
To Thee be praise;
Teach me by faith
To keep Thy ways.

CRUNCHY PEANUT BUTTER SQUARES

¾ cup corn syrup
¾ cup firmly packed brown sugar
¾ cup peanut butter
6 cups KELLOGG'S RICE KRISPIES cereal

1. Mix corn syrup and sugar together in large saucepan. Cook over medium heat, stirring often, until mixture is bubbly.
2. After removing from heat, add peanut butter. Mix well. Add cereal and stir.
3. Grease hands or use waxed paper and press mixture into greased 13 x 9 x 2 inch pan. Cool. Cut into 24 squares.

One example is worth a thousand precepts.

RICE KRISPY FAVORITES

    ¼ **cup margarine**
    1 **ten-ounce package (about 40)**
      regular marshmallows or
    4 **cups miniature marshmallows**
    5 **cups KELLOGG'S RICE KRISPIES cereal**

1. Melt margarine in large, heavy saucepan.
2. Add marshmallows. Cook and stir over low heat until marshmallows melt. Mix well. Remove from heat.
3. Stir in cereal until well coated.
4. Press while warm into greased 13 x 9 x 2 inch pan. Cool. Cut into 24 squares.

Variations: Add 1 cup salted peanuts with cereal.

Add ½ cup coconut.

Add 1 cup raisins or dates.

Substitute KELLOGG'S COCOA KRISPIES cereal for KELLOGG'S RICE KRISPIES cereal.

Add ½ cup crushed peppermint candy or other hard candy.

Stir ¼ cup peanut butter into warm marshmallow mixture. Blend well before adding cereal.

Melt 2 squares unsweetened chocolate with marshmallows. Blend well.

5

Desserts

APPLE CRISP

    5 medium-size cooking apples, cored and sliced
  ⅓ cup sifted all-purpose flour
    1 teaspoon cinnamon
  ½ cup firmly packed brown sugar
1½ cups granola
  ⅓ cup melted margarine

1. Put apple slices in greased 9 x 9 x 2 inch baking pan.
2. Mix flour, cinnamon, sugar, and cereal. Add melted margarine. Mix well.
3. Sprinkle mixture over apple slices.
4. Bake at 350°F. about 25 minutes. Serve warm or cold with milk, cream, ice cream, or whipped topping. Serves 8 to 10.

Could I climb to the highest place in Athens, I would lift my voice and proclaim: "Fellow citizens, why do ye turn and scrape every stone to gather wealth and take so little care of your children, to whom one day you must relinquish it all?"
           SOCRATES

CHEESY APPLE CRISP

4 medium apples
½ cup margarine
¾ cup firmly packed brown sugar
½ cup all-purpose flour
½ teaspoon cinnamon
¾ cup bran flakes
grated cheddar cheese to taste

1. Peel, core, and slice apples. Arrange in 8 x 8 x 2 inch baking dish.
2. Cream margarine. Add brown sugar, flour, and cinnamon, and mix well.
3. Stir in cereal and sprinkle mixture over apples.
4. Bake at 375°F. for about 30 minutes. While still warm, sprinkle with grated cheddar cheese.

CRACKLIN' BRAN APPLE CRISP

1 cup KELLOGG'S CRACKLIN' BRAN cereal
½ cup all-purpose flour
¾ teaspoon cinnamon
½ teaspoon nutmeg
⅔ cup firmly packed brown sugar
⅓ cup softened margarine
4 cups sliced, peeled apples

1. Crush cereal and place in mixing bowl.
2. Stir in flour, cinnamon, nutmeg, and brown sugar.
3. Add margarine and mix until crumbly.
4. Place sliced apples in greased 8 x 8 x 2 inch pan or 2 quart casserole. Sprinkle crumbly mixture over top.
5. Bake at 375°F. about 30 minutes, until apples are tender and topping is browned. Serve warm, with or without cream, whipped topping, or ice cream. Serves 6.

Like apples of gold in settings of silver
Is a word spoken in right circumstances.   PROVERBS 25:11

APPLESAUCE CRUNCH

½ cup butter or margarine
4 cups GOLDEN GRAHAMS
  breakfast cereal, crushed
2½ cups applesauce
1 teaspoon cinnamon
¼ teaspoon salt
1 cup chilled whipping cream
¼ cup sugar

1. Melt butter or margarine in skillet. Stir in cereal. Heat together about 5 minutes, until cereal begins to brown.
2. In small bowl, mix applesauce, cinnamon, and salt.
3. Sprinkle half the cereal mixture over the bottom of a greased 8 or 9 inch, square pan.
4. Spread half the applesauce over the cereal mixture.
5. Add another layer of cereal mixture, the last half of the applesauce, and a final layer of cereal mixture.
6. Whip cream, adding sugar gradually to whipped cream. Spread over top. Refrigerate at least 3 hours. Serves 9 to 12.

STUFFED BAKED APPLES

4 large baking apples
⅓ cup POST GRAPE-NUTS brand cereal
⅓ cup firmly packed brown sugar
2 tablespoons softened margarine
½ teaspoon cinnamon
½ cup raisins

1. Core apples and peel skin from top half of each. Put into small baking dish.
2. Mix cereal, sugar, margarine, and cinnamon in small bowl.
3. Put alternate layers of cereal mixture and raisins into center of each apple.
4. Pour water into pan just to cover bottom.
5. Bake, uncovered, at 400°F. for 50 to 60 minutes, basting with syrup in dish, until apples are tender.
6. Serve warm or cool, with cream, if desired. Serves 4.

Great God, Thou giver of all good,
Accept our praise and bless this food,
Grace, health, and strength to us afford,
Through Jesus Christ, our risen Lord.

GOLDEN GRAHAMS-APPLE CRUMBLE

4 cups sliced, peeled baking apples
(about 4 medium-size apples)
3 cups GOLDEN GRAHAMS breakfast cereal, crushed
⅔ cup firmly packed brown sugar
⅓ cup softened margarine

1. Place sliced apples in greased 8 x 8 x 2 inch baking pan.
2. Mix cereal, brown sugar, and margarine until crumbly. Sprinkle over apples.
3. Bake at 375°F. about 30 to 40 minutes, until apples are tender. Serve with cream or whipped topping, if desired. Serves 9.

BLUEBERRY CASSEROLE

1 cup granola, crushed slightly
¼ cup sugar
¼ teaspoon cinnamon
3 tablespoons melted margarine
2 cups fresh or frozen blueberries
whipped topping

1. In small bowl, mix cereal, sugar, and cinnamon.
2. Add melted margarine and stir well.
3. Put 1 cup blueberries in greased 1 quart casserole. Cover with half the cereal mixture. Add rest of blueberries, then rest of cereal mixture. Press down firmly.
4. Bake at 350°F. for about 30 minutes. Cool. Cut in squares. Top with whipped topping. Serves 4 to 6.

SOUR CREAM-APPLE DESSERT

2 cups CORN CHEX cereal, crushed to 1 cup
1 cup sifted all-purpose flour
2 cups firmly packed brown sugar
½ cup softened margarine
1 cup chopped walnuts
1 cup dairy sour cream
1 slightly beaten egg
½ teaspoon cinnamon
1 teaspoon baking soda
½ teaspoon salt
1 teaspoon vanilla
2 cups peeled, cored, and finely chopped apples

1. In large bowl, mix cereal, flour, sugar, and margarine. Blend in mixer at low speed until crumbly.
2. Stir in nuts.
3. Spread 2¾ cups of this mixture evenly in ungreased 13 x 9 x 2 inch baking pan.
4. To rest of mixture add cream, egg, cinnamon, soda, salt, and vanilla. Beat well.
5. Add apples and stir. Put in baking pan on top of first mixture.
6. Bake at 350°F. about 30 to 40 minutes, until pick inserted near center comes out clean. Can be served warm or cool, with or without cream, or whipped topping. Serves 12 to 15.

Give a little love to a child, and you get a great deal back.

JOHN RUSKIN

I love you for what you are, but I love you yet more for what you are going to be. CARL SANDBURG

MARASCHINO CHERRY DESSERT

½ cup softened margarine
3 tablespoons sifted confectioners' sugar
½ cup all-purpose flour
½ cup finely crushed cornflakes
¼ cup all-purpose flour
½ teaspoon baking powder
¼ teaspoon salt
2 eggs
1 cup granulated sugar
1 teaspoon vanilla
½ cup coarsely chopped nuts
½ cup flaked coconut
½ cup finely chopped maraschino cherries
whipped topping or vanilla ice cream

1. Beat margarine and confectioners' sugar together in small mixing bowl until creamy.
2. Stir in ½ cup flour and crushed flakes.
3. Spread in bottom of 8 x 8 x 2 inch pan. Bake at 325°F. about 20 minutes.
4. Combine ¼ cup flour, baking powder, and salt in small bowl.
5. Beat eggs slightly in medium-size bowl. Add sugar and vanilla, and stir. Add flour mixture. Mix well. Add nuts, coconut, and maraschino cherries. Stir. Spread over baked crust.
6. Bake at 325°F. for 30 to 40 minutes, until light brown. Cool. Cut into 9 large or 12 small pieces. Serve with ice cream or whipped topping.

HONEY-NUT BAKED APPLES

   6 **large apples**
   ⅓ **cup honey**
   ⅓ **cup granola**
   ⅓ **cup chopped dates**
   ¼ **cup chopped walnuts**
   ½ **teaspoon cinnamon**
   ¼ **teaspoon nutmeg**
   2 **teaspoons lemon juice**
   3 **tablespoons melted margarine**
   ¾ **cup apple juice or water**
      cream or ice cream

1. Core apples and stand in 9 x 9 x 2 inch baking dish.
2. Mix 3 tablespoons of the honey with the granola, dates, walnuts, cinnamon, nutmeg, and lemon juice. Spoon into center of each apple.
3. Combine rest of honey, melted margarine, and juice or water. Pour over apples.
4. Cover and bake at 350°F. for 30 minutes. Remove cover and bake about 35 more minutes, basting frequently with juices from baking dish, until apples are tender.
5. Serve warm or cool with cream or ice cream. Serves 6.

CHERRY-PINEAPPLE DESSERT

    1 sixteen-ounce can pitted, red, tart cherries, water pack
    1 eight-ounce can crushed pineapple, in syrup
    ⅓ cup sugar
    3 tablespoons quick-cooking tapioca
      dash of salt
    ¾ cup granola
    ½ cup all-purpose flour
    ¼ cup sugar
    ½ teaspoon cinnamon
    3 tablespoons melted margarine

1. Drain liquid from fruits and set aside.
2. Mix ⅓ cup sugar, the tapioca, and salt in heavy saucepan. Add liquids from canned fruits. Cook to full boil over medium heat, stirring constantly.
3. Remove from heat and add fruit. Put in 1½ quart baking dish.
4. Mix cereal, flour, ¼ cup sugar, and cinnamon. Add margarine and mix. Spread over fruit mixture. Bake at 375°F. for 20 to 25 minutes, until light brown. Serve warm with cream or ice cream, if desired. Serves 6 to 8.

You cannot kindle a fire in any other heart until it is burning within your own.

PEACH BETTY

    4 cups sliced, peeled, fresh peaches (8 medium)
    ½ cup all-purpose flour
    ¼ cup firmly packed brown sugar
    ½ teaspoon cinnamon
    ¼ teaspoon nutmeg
    ¼ cup margarine
    ¾ cup granola

1. Arrange sliced peaches in shallow 1½ quart baking dish.
2. Combine flour, sugar, cinnamon, and nutmeg in medium-size bowl. Cut in margarine. Stir in cereal. Sprinkle mixture over peaches.
3. Bake at 375°F. for 30 minutes. Serves 8 to 10.
   Variation: Substitute 1 twenty-nine-ounce can sliced peaches and 1 sixteen-ounce can pear halves, sliced, with ¼ cup syrup from drained fruit for the fresh peaches.

DATE DESSERT

CRUMBS
¾ cup softened margarine
½ cup sugar
1 cup firmly packed brown sugar
1½ cups sifted all-purpose flour
8 cups RICE CHEX cereal, crushed to 4 cups

FILLING
¾ cup boiling water
2 cups finely chopped, pitted dates
1 cup light corn syrup
3 slightly beaten eggs
⅓ cup firmly packed brown sugar
3 tablespoons sifted all-purpose flour

1. Cream margarine and both kinds of sugar in large bowl. Add sifted flour. Mix well. Stir in cereal crumbs.
2. Press 4 cups of the cereal mixture into bottom of greased 13 x 9 x 2 inch pan. Reserve rest for topping.
3. For filling, pour water over chopped dates. Allow to stand for five minutes. Mix in corn syrup, beaten eggs, brown sugar, and flour.
4. Spread date mixture over crust. Sprinkle rest of cereal mixture over top. Press lightly.
5. Bake at 350°F. for 40 to 45 minutes. Serve either warm or cool, with or without ice cream. Serves 12 to 16.

BAKED PEARS

4 to 6 large pears
⅔ cup granola
⅔ cup firmly packed brown sugar
¼ cup melted margarine
½ teaspoon nutmeg
¼ teaspoon salt

1. Wash, core, and peel large, whole pears.
2. Mix together cereal, sugar, melted margarine, nutmeg, and salt.
3. Spoon mixture into centers of pears. Place in shallow baking dish. Add water to cover bottom.
4. Bake uncovered at 400°F. for 30 minutes. Serve with syrup from baking dish or with chocolate sauce. Serves 4 to 6.

For food and friends
And all God sends
We give Him thanks.
AMEN.

FROZEN CHOCOLATE DESSERT

  4 cups **RICE CHEX** cereal, crushed to 1¼ cups
  ¼ cup firmly packed brown sugar
  6 tablespoons melted margarine
  3 cups sifted confectioners' sugar
  3 tablespoons cocoa
  ¼ teaspoon salt
  ¾ cup margarine
  2 eggs
  1 cup chopped pecans
1½ teaspoons vanilla
1½ cups thawed, non-dairy whipped topping

1. Place cereal crumbs in shallow baking pan. Toast at 350°F. about 10 minutes, until lightly browned.
2. Mix together toasted crumbs, brown sugar, and melted margarine. Reserve ¼ cup and press the rest into bottom of greased 9 x 9 x 2 inch pan. Chill about 1 hour.
3. Combine confectioners' sugar, cocoa, and salt in small bowl.
4. Cream margarine in large bowl. Beat in confectioners' sugar mixture and cream until fluffy. Add eggs one at a time, beating 5 minutes after each addition.
5. Add nuts and vanilla. Fold in whipped topping.
6. Pour into pan over cereal crust. Sprinkle the reserved ¼ cup of cereal mixture over top. Cover.
7. Freeze at least 6 hours. Serves 12 to 16.

Persons are to be loved; things are to be used.   REUEL HOWE

FROZEN LEMON FROTH

2½ cups **WHEATIES** breakfast cereal,
   finely crushed to make ¾ cup
3 **eggs, separated**
½ **cup sugar**
1 **cup whipping cream**
1 **tablespoon grated lemon rind**
¼ **cup lemon juice**

1. Grease a refrigerator tray well. Press half the cereal crumbs onto bottom of tray.
2. Beat egg whites until they hold their shape. Gradually beat in sugar. Continue beating until stiff and glossy.
3. Beat egg yolks until thick. Fold into egg white mixture.
4. Whip together cream, lemon rind, and lemon juice until thick. Fold into egg mixture.
5. Pour into tray. Sprinkle rest of crumbs on top. Freeze. Cut into squares or slices. Serves 8 to 10.

BERRY SUNDAES

3 **cups puffed rice**
1½ **cups fresh or frozen blueberries,**
   thawed and drained
3 **cups puffed wheat**
1½ **cups sliced fresh or frozen strawberries,**
   thawed and drained
6 **scoops of sherbet or ice cream**

1. Set out 6 cereal bowls.
2. In each bowl, alternate layers of puffed rice, blueberries, puffed wheat, and strawberries.
3. Top each with scoop of sherbet or ice cream. Serves 6.
   Variation: Put sherbet or ice cream on bottom. Top with any desired combination of the cereals and berries listed.

FROZEN PEANUT BUTTER CRUNCH

CRUST
2½ cups granola, coarsely crushed
¼ cup peanut butter
¼ cup honey

FILLING
¼ cup peanut butter
¼ cup honey
1½ quarts vanilla ice cream, softened

1. Crush cereal into coarse pieces.
2. Put peanut butter and honey for crust in medium-size saucepan. Melt over low heat. Stir in cereal.
3. Cover bottom and sides of 9 x 9 x 2 inch baking pan with aluminum foil, leaving foil extending over the edges. Brush foil with cooking oil.
4. Press two-thirds crust mixture onto bottom of pan. Chill.
5. Mix peanut butter and honey for filling. Swirl through softened vanilla ice cream. Spoon into baking dish on top of crust mixture. Sprinkle remaining crust mixture over top.
6. Place in freezer for 3 to 4 hours. Set out about 5 minutes before serving. Cut into squares. Serves 12 to 16.

"Charlie, you can do almost anything with a child if you love him enough."   CHARLIE SHEDD, quoting his father-in-law

---

PECAN-BUTTERSCOTCH ICE CREAM

¼ cup butter
6 tablespoons brown sugar
½ cup chopped pecans
2 cups WHEATIES breakfast cereal
1 quart vanilla ice cream

1. Put butter and brown sugar in heavy saucepan. Cook together until thick, stirring constantly.
2. Add chopped nuts and cereal.
3. Spread mixture out on baking sheet. Cool and then crumble.
4. Soften vanilla ice cream. Stir crumbled mixture into ice cream. Put in freezer tray or other container and freeze until firm. Serves 6.

ICE CREAM SQUARES

4 cups GOLDEN GRAHAMS
breakfast cereal, crushed
1 cup flaked coconut
¼ cup chopped nuts
¼ cup melted margarine
¼ cup honey
1 quart vanilla ice cream, softened

1. Combine cereal, coconut, nuts, melted margarine, and honey in large bowl.
2. Press two-thirds of this mixture into bottom of ungreased 9 x 9 x 2 inch pan.
3. Press softened ice cream evenly over bottom layer.
4. Sprinkle rest of cereal mixture over top.
5. Freeze overnight. Serves 9.

We thank Thee, Father, for Thy care,
And for Thy bounty everywhere;
For this and every other gift,
Our grateful hearts to Thee we lift.

ICE CREAM SANDWICHES

½ cup light corn syrup
½ cup peanut butter
4 cups KELLOGG'S RICE KRISPIES cereal
1 pint ice cream

1. Combine corn syrup and peanut butter in medium-size bowl. Stir in cereal.
2. Press cereal mixture into greased 13 x 9 x 2 inch jelly roll pan. Put in freezer until firm.
3. Cut into twelve 3-inch squares. Cut ice cream into 6 slices of similar shape.
4. Put one slice of ice cream between 2 squares. Repeat, making 6 sandwiches. Wrap each in foil. Keep in freezer until served.

WINTER COBBLER

⅔ cup finely crushed cornflakes
½ cup chopped pecans
1 teaspoon cinnamon
¼ teaspoon nutmeg
1 twenty-nine-ounce can pear halves
1 eight-ounce can crushed pineapple, drained
½ cup seedless raisins
1 nine-ounce package white or yellow cake mix
⅓ cup melted margarine

1. Mix cereal crumbs, nuts, cinnamon, and nutmeg in small bowl.
2. Drain pears. Measure ⅓ cup syrup. Cut pears into small pieces.
3. Mix pears, pineapple, and raisins. Spread out in lightly greased 9 x 9 x 2 inch pan.
4. Sprinkle dry cake mix over fruit. Drizzle the ⅓ cup pear syrup over top. Sprinkle cereal mixture on top and pour melted margarine evenly over that.
5. Bake at 350°F. about 50 minutes, until top is crisp and light brown. Serve warm or cool, with cream, ice cream, or whipped topping, if desired. Serves 9.

The tongue of the wise makes knowledge acceptable. PROVERBS 15:2

BANANA SUNDAE

1 cup slightly crushed CORN CHEX cereal
1 sliced banana
½ cup softened ice cream

1. Put ¾ cup crushed cereal in bottom of dish.
2. Arrange sliced bananas over cereal.
3. Top with chocolate ice cream and rest of cereal.
   Variations: RICE CHEX cereal, strawberries, and vanilla ice cream; WHEAT CHEX cereal, bananas, and butter brickle ice cream; or CORN CHEX cereal, blueberries, and vanilla ice cream.

REFRIGERATOR ICE CREAM

½ cup sugar
4 teaspoons flour
⅛ teaspoon salt
1 cup scalded milk
1 cup heavy cream, whipped
1 teaspoon vanilla
2 tablespoons margarine
3 tablespoons brown sugar
1 cup cornflakes
¼ cup chopped nuts

1. Combine sugar, flour, and salt in large saucepan.
2. Stir scalded milk into dry ingredients. Cook over low heat about 20 minutes, until thickened slightly. Cool.
3. Fold in whipped cream and vanilla. Pour into refrigerator tray. Freeze.
4. Melt margarine in medium-size saucepan over low heat. Add brown sugar. Stirring constantly, cook until thick and smooth. Add cereal and nuts. Blend well and allow to cool.
5. Put frozen ice cream into a chilled bowl. Beat with cold beater until smooth and light. Fold in cereal and nut mixture. Put back in refrigerator tray and freeze. Serves 6.

FROZEN CHEERIOS DESSERT

1 **package chocolate malt frosting mix**
¼ **cup margarine**
3 **tablespoons hot water**
½ **teaspoon vanilla**
½ **cup peanuts**
3 **cups CHEERIOS breakfast cereal**

1. Blend dry frosting mix, margarine, hot water, and vanilla in large bowl.
2. Stir in peanuts and cereal.
3. Spread in greased 9 x 9 x 2 inch pan and cover. Freeze a few hours until firm. Cut into squares just before serving. Serve frozen. Serves 16.

Father, send Thy blessing,
Gently as the dew;
May thy gracious presence
Keep us strong and true.

CHOCOLATE-PEPPERMINT CUPS

1 **cup slightly crushed**
   KELLOGG'S RICE KRISPIES cereal
⅓ **cup flaked coconut**
¼ **cup finely chopped walnuts**
1 **cup chocolate chips**
6 **paper bake cups**
   peppermint ice cream

1. Mix together cereal, coconut, and nuts.
2. Melt chocolate in top of double boiler over hot water.
3. Pour chocolate over cereal mixture. Stir well.
4. Put paper baking cups into 6 muffin cups. Press ⅓ cup cereal mixture onto bottom and sides of each cup. Chill in refrigerator.
5. Take out of refrigerator 15 minutes before serving time. Just before serving, fill each shell with peppermint ice cream.
   Variation: Use chocolate shower ice cream or vanilla ice cream.

CRUNCHY LEMON PUDDING

2 tablespoons margarine
½ cup POST GRAPE-NUTS brand cereal
¼ cup firmly packed brown sugar
1 small package lemon pudding mix

1. Melt margarine in medium-size saucepan. Stir in cereal and sugar. Set aside.
2. Prepare lemon pudding according to package directions.
3. Put ⅓ cereal mixture in bottoms of individual dessert dishes, then half the lemon pudding. Repeat, and top each dish with rest of cereal.
4. Chill. Serves 6.

We learn that God has created each one of us for a special work and place in the world; He has a definite plan for each little life. He knows each child individually and by name. It is good to know that we are very precious in His sight.   ELSIE D. HOLSINGER

CEREAL PARFAITS

chilled pudding
granola

1. Prepare any desired kind of pudding and chill thoroughly, covering surface of cooked pudding with plastic wrap.
2. Stir pudding. Alternately put layers of pudding and granola into parfait glasses. Serve at once.

An ounce of illustration is worth a ton of talk.

RICH COCONUT DESSERT

    2 cups CORN CHEX cereal, crushed to ¾ cup
1½ teaspoons and 1 cup sugar
    1 tablespoon and ½ cup margarine
    2 eggs
  ½ teaspoon vanilla
    1 cup sifted all-purpose flour
    1 teaspoon baking powder
  ⅛ teaspoon salt
    1 cup flaked coconut
       confectioners' sugar

1. Mix cereal crumbs and 1½ teaspoons sugar. Melt
1 tablespoon margarine and stir into cereal mixture.
Set aside.
2. Cream ½ cup margarine and 1 cup sugar in medium-size
bowl. Beat in eggs and vanilla until creamy.
3. Sift together flour, baking powder, and salt. Add this and
coconut to creamed mixture. Mix well.
4. Pour batter into greased 9 x 9 x 2 inch pan. Sprinkle
cereal mixture over top and press lightly into batter.
5. Bake at 350°F. about 35 minutes, until light brown around
edges. Dust with confectioners' sugar. Cool 10 minutes.
Cut into 9 squares. Serve warm with whipped topping or
ice cream.

We bring to thee the children, Heavenly Father. Their faults will wear away, but their lovable qualities will grow more beautiful every day, under Thy Fatherly guidance. Amen.   AMOS R. WELLS

PINEAPPLE-COTTAGE CHEESECAKE

CRUST
      1 cup crushed cornflakes
      ¼ cup sugar
      6 tablespoons melted margarine

FILLING
      1 envelope unflavored gelatin
      ¼ cup cold water
      3 egg yolks
      1 cup crushed pineapple and juice
      1 tablespoon lemon juice
      ¼ cup sugar
      ½ teaspoon salt
      1 cup cottage cheese
      3 egg whites
      ½ cup sugar

1. Mix together cereal, sugar, and melted margarine. Press into bottom of a 9 x 9 x 2 inch baking pan.
2. Soak gelatin in cold water.
3. Beat egg yolks. Add pineapple with liquid, lemon juice, ¼ cup sugar, and salt. Cook in double boiler over hot water, stirring constantly. When thick, remove from heat and stir in the softened gelatin. Cool until it starts to thicken.
4. Put cottage cheese through wire strainer. Stir it into pineapple mixture.
5. Beat egg whites until stiff. Add ½ cup sugar slowly, while beating.
6. Fold egg whites into pineapple mixture. Pour over crust. Chill until firm.

EASY CHOCOLATE PARFAIT

>   1 **six-ounce package (1 cup) chocolate chips**
>   3 **cups granola**
>   1 **quart vanilla, chocolate, or**
>   **chocolate ripple ice cream**

1. Melt chocolate chips in top of double boiler over hot water.
2. Stir in cereal. Coat well.
3. Spread out in thin layer on cookie sheet covered with waxed paper. Chill until firm. Break into small pieces.
4. Spoon half the ice cream into 8 parfait glasses. Next put 3 to 4 tablespoons of cereal mixture in each glass. Repeat with rest of ice cream and rest of cereal.
5. Serve immediately or place in freezer until ready to serve. Serves 8.

First I learned to love my teacher, then I learned to love my teacher's Bible, then I learned to love my teacher's Saviour.

MARION LAWRENCE

BANANA SPLITS

>   6 **bananas, sliced in half lengthwise**
>   1 **pint chocolate ice cream**
>   1 **pint vanilla ice cream**
>   1 **pint strawberry ice cream**
>   ¾ **cup granola**
>   **strawberry topping**
>   **fudge topping**

1. Place 1 banana on each serving dish.
2. Arrange on banana 1 scoop of chocolate ice cream, 1 of vanilla ice cream, and 1 of strawberry ice cream.
3. Spoon strawberry and fudge topping over top.
4. Sprinkle with cereal. Serves 6.

BRAN CUSTARD

> 3 eggs
> 2 cups milk
> ⅛ teaspoon salt
> ⅛ teaspoon nutmeg
> ½ cup sugar
> 1 teaspoon vanilla
> 1 cup KELLOGG'S CRACKLIN' BRAN cereal
> ⅓ cup seedless raisins

1. Beat eggs until foamy, using medium-size bowl.
2. Mix in milk, salt, nutmeg, sugar, vanilla, cereal, and raisins.
3. Pour into 6 buttered custard cups or one 1½ quart glass casserole dish.
4. Place custard cups or casserole in large baking pan and put about 1 inch of hot water in pan.
5. Bake at 375°F. about 45 minutes, until knife inserted near center comes out clean.
6. Serve warm. Serves 6.
   Variation: Add ½ cup finely chopped nuts.

If you train up a child to give pennies, when he is old he will not depart from it.

FROZEN CRUNCH BALLS

> 1 pint ice cream, any desired flavor
> 1 cup slightly crushed granola

1. Form 4 ice cream balls from 1 pint of ice cream. Place on cold cookie sheet in freezer.
2. When ice cream balls are firm, roll them in cereal and return to freezer. Again freeze until firm.
3. Serve with sundae topping, if desired, or with fruit for a fruit plate. Serves 4.

RICE CHEX CHEESECAKE

4 cups RICE CHEX cereal, crushed to 1 cup
¼ cup firmly packed brown sugar
⅛ teaspoon nutmeg
⅓ cup melted margarine
2 eight-ounce packages softened cream cheese
2 cups milk
2 cups dairy sour cream
2 three-and-three-quarter-ounce packages
   vanilla instant pudding
1 teaspoon grated lemon peel

1. Mix together cereal, sugar, and nutmeg. Add melted margarine and stir. Reserve ¼ cup cereal mixture for topping. Press remainder into bottom of greased 9-inch spring form pan.
2. Spread topping crumbs in shallow pan.
3. Bake both cereal mixtures at 300°F. about 10 minutes.
4. Beat cream cheese at medium speed until creamy. Add milk slowly, mixing in each addition. Add sour cream, pudding mix, and lemon peel. Beat until smooth.
5. Pour into pan on top of cereal mixture. Sprinkle topping crumbs over top. Chill 3 to 4 hours. Serves 8 to 10.

Every child is entitled to a heritage of happy memories, entirely independent of riches or poverty. The far-reaching influence of early impressions will be in proportion to the adult companionship unselfishly given children in their formative years. Stored-up recollections will enrich and help mold manhood and womanhood. ELSIE D. HOLSINGER

STRAWBERRY PARFAITS

1 quart vanilla ice cream
2 ten-ounce packages frozen,
   sliced strawberries, partially thawed
2 cups sugar frosted cornflakes

1. Set out 8 parfait glasses.
2. In each glass, put about ¼ cup ice cream, 3 tablespoons strawberries, and ¼ cup cornflakes.
3. Top with another ¼ cup ice cream and a few strawberries. Serves 8.

COCONUT-PEANUT TOPPING

3 tablespoons margarine
¼ cup firmly packed brown sugar
½ cup flaked coconut
½ cup salted cocktail peanuts
2 cups KELLOGG'S PRODUCT 19 cereal

1. In medium-size saucepan, melt margarine and stir in sugar. While stirring constantly, cook over medium heat until mixture comes to full boil.
2. Remove from stove and add coconut, peanuts, and cereal. Stir well.
3. Spread on cookie sheet covered with waxed paper. Cool. Makes 3 cups cereal topping that can be stored, covered, in refrigerator.

O give us hearts to thank Thee,
For every blessing sent
And whatsoever Thou sendest
Make us therewith content.

CARAMEL TOPPING

½ cup margarine
1¼ cups finely crushed cornflakes
¾ cup firmly packed brown sugar
¾ cup shredded coconut
½ cup coarsely chopped nuts
¼ cup all-purpose flour
¼ teaspoon cinnamon
¼ teaspoon nutmeg

1. Melt margarine in medium-size saucepan over low heat. Stir in cereal, sugar, coconut, nuts, flour, cinnamon, and nutmeg.
2. Spread mixture on 2 ungreased cookie sheets.
3. Bake at 350°F. about 12 minutes, until light brown and crisp. Stir a couple of times during baking. Cool.
4. Store tightly covered. Use as topping for puddings and ice cream. Makes 4 cups.

GOLDEN HONEY DESSERT TOPPING

4 cups GOLDEN GRAHAMS breakfast cereal
½ cup chopped nuts, if desired
2 tablespoons margarine
1 cup honey

1. Combine cereal and nuts in large, greased bowl.
2. Melt margarine in heavy pan over medium heat. Stir in honey. Stirring constantly, cook to brittle stage (300°F.).
3. Pour syrup over cereal mixture and stir.
4. Quickly spread out on cookie sheet. Cool well.
5. Break up and crush with rolling pin. Roll out quite fine. Store tightly covered. Use on pudding, fruit, or ice cream. Makes about 3½ cups.

I think that one of the best things to do for our children is to help them find and believe in their potentials.   RUTH PEALE

PEANUT BUTTER TOPPING

¼ cup peanut butter
¼ cup margarine
1 cup firmly packed brown sugar
2 cups coarsely crushed cornflakes
1 cup salted peanuts

1. Stir together peanut butter, margarine, and sugar in medium-size saucepan. Stir over low heat until bubbly. Cook 2 to 3 more minutes. Remove from heat.
2. Add cereal and peanuts. Mix well.
3. Spread on greased cookie sheet. Cool. Store tightly covered. Use as needed on pudding and ice cream. Makes about 3 cups.

COCONUT TOPPING

3 tablespoons margarine
¼ cup corn syrup
2 cups KELLOGG'S RICE KRISPIES cereal
½ cup flaked coconut
½ cup nuts

1. Combine margarine and corn syrup in medium-size saucepan. Stirring often, cook over medium heat to boiling point. Remove from heat.
2. Stir in cereal, coconut, and nuts.
3. Spread quickly on waxed paper or greased cookie sheet. Cool. Break into small pieces. Store loosely covered. Serve over pudding or ice cream. Makes about 3 cups.

We pray thee, Lord, that we may feel
Thy presence with us at this meal,
And when we leave may we have fed
On fellowship as well as bread.
AMEN.

FRANCES MYERS

BRAN-NUT TOPPING

2 tablespoons margarine
¼ cup firmly packed brown sugar
1 cup bran flakes
⅔ cup coconut
¼ cup chopped pecans

1. Melt margarine in large skillet over low heat. Add brown sugar. Blend well.
2. Add cereal, coconut, and pecans. Stir over medium heat until cereal is lightly browned.
3. Remove from heat, and cool.
4. Store in covered container for use as topping for frosted cake or ice cream. Makes about 2 cups.

6

Main Dishes

GRAPE-NUTS MEAT LOAF

   ½ cup POST GRAPE-NUTS brand cereal
   ½ cup water
   1 pound ground beef
   1 slightly beaten egg
   2 teaspoons Worcestershire sauce
   ¼ cup finely chopped onion
   ¾ teaspoon salt
   ⅛ teaspoon pepper
   ¼ cup catsup

1. Mix cereal and water. Allow to stand about 1 minute.
2. Add ground beef, egg, Worcestershire sauce, onion, salt, and pepper. Mix well.
3. Press into greased loaf pan. Spread catsup over top.
4. Bake at 350°F. about 1 hour. Serves 6.

The first impressions remain to the last, both in the memory and on the mind. Let every teacher of the very young ask for grace to be very wise.
CHARLES H. SPURGEON

BARBECUE-FLAVORED MEAT LOAF

    1 slightly beaten egg
    ¼ cup and 3 tablespoons barbecue sauce
    1 tablespoon Worcestershire sauce
    2 teaspoons seasoned salt
    ¼ teaspoon garlic powder
    1½ cups BRAN CHEX cereal
    1½ pounds lean ground beef
    ⅓ cup finely chopped onion
    ¼ cup finely chopped green pepper

1. Combine slightly beaten egg, ¼ cup barbecue sauce, Worcestershire sauce, salt, and garlic powder in large bowl.
2. Add cereal and stir until coated. Let stand a few minutes. Stir again to break up cereal slightly.
3. Add ground beef, onion, and pepper. Stir well.
4. Form loaf in loaf pan. Bake at 350°F. about 65 minutes. Take from oven and spread 3 tablespoons barbecue sauce over top. Bake 10 minutes more. Serves 6.

RICE KRISPIES MEAT LOAF

    1 egg
    ¾ cup milk
    1 teaspoon salt
    ⅛ teaspoon pepper
    1 teaspoon dry mustard
    1 tablespoon Worcestershire sauce
    ⅓ cup finely chopped onion
    2 cups KELLOGG'S RICE KRISPIES cereal
    1½ pounds lean ground beef

1. Beat together in large bowl the egg, milk, salt, pepper, mustard, Worcestershire sauce, and onion.
2. Add cereal and stir. Let stand 5 minutes. Beat well.
3. Add ground beef and stir. Press into greased loaf pan.
4. Bake at 350°F. about 1 hour, until browned and well cooked. Serves 8.
   Variation: Shape into patties. Place in greased baking pan and bake at 350°F. about 25 minutes. For cheeseburgers, place cheese slice on each patty and return to oven briefly. Serve on plain or toasted hamburger buns. Serves 6 to 8.

Of all commentaries upon the Scriptures, good examples are the best and liveliest.   JOHN DONNE

MINIATURE MEAT LOAVES

   1 **pound ground beef**
   ½ **pound ground pork**
   2 **eggs, slightly beaten**
   ¾ **cup chopped onion**
   2 **tablespoons chopped parsley**
   ½ **teaspoon crushed bay leaf**
   ½ **teaspoon ground thyme**
   ½ **teaspoon salt**
   ¾ **cup crushed WHEATIES breakfast cereal**
   ⅛ **teaspoon pepper**
   1½ **cups whole WHEATIES breakfast cereal**

1. Combine ground meats, eggs, onion, parsley, bay leaf, thyme, salt, ¾ cup crushed cereal, and pepper in large bowl.
2. Form into 3-inch loaves. Roll in whole cereal flakes.
3. Bake in 8 x 8 x 2 inch pan at 350°F. about 35 minutes. Makes 8 individual loaves.

APPLESAUCE MEATBALLS

   1 **pound ground beef**
   1 **slightly beaten egg**
   ¼ **cup applesauce**
   ½ **cup crushed cornflakes**
   ½ **cup chopped onion**
   ¾ **teaspoon salt**
   ⅛ **teaspoon pepper**
   ⅛ **teaspoon garlic salt**
   1 **eight-ounce can tomato sauce**

1. Combine meat, egg, applesauce, cereal, onion, salt, pepper, and garlic salt in large bowl. Mix well.
2. Shape into small balls. Put in baking dish.
3. Pour tomato sauce over top. Bake at 350°F. for 1 hour. Serves 4 to 6.

Our table now with food is spread;
O Lord who giveth daily bread,
Bless these Thy gifts unto us so
That strength of body they bestow.

ORIENTAL MEATBALLS

½ cup POST GRAPE-NUTS brand cereal
½ cup water
1 pound ground beef
¼ cup finely chopped onion
2 tablespoons soy sauce
1 teaspoon salt
⅛ teaspoon pepper
2 tablespoons oil
2 tablespoons cornstarch
½ cup water
½ cup sweet pickle chips
¼ cup sweet pickle liquid
1 fifteen-and-a-quarter-ounce
   can pineapple chunks
6 servings rice

1. Mix cereal and ½ cup water in large bowl. Let stand 1 minute.
2. Add meat, onion, soy sauce, salt, and pepper.
3. Form into small balls and brown in hot oil.
4. Mix cornstarch and ½ cup water.
5. Combine pickle chips, pickle liquid, pineapple with juice, and cornstarch mixture. Pour over meatballs.
6. Bring to a boil, stirring constantly. Cook until sauce is thick and clear.
7. Prepare either quick-cooking or regular rice as directed on package.
8. Pour meatballs with sauce over rice just before serving. Serves 6.

SAUCY MEATBALLS

MEATBALLS

1 egg
1 cup KELLOGG'S RICE KRISPIES cereal
¼ cup finely chopped onion
⅔ cup instant nonfat dry
milk (in dry form)
2 tablespoons catsup
1 teaspoon salt
⅛ teaspoon pepper
1 pound ground beef

SAUCE

1 fifteen-ounce can tomato sauce
½ cup catsup
½ cup water
¼ cup firmly packed brown sugar
¼ cup finely chopped onion
¼ cup pickle relish
2 tablespoons Worcestershire sauce
1 tablespoon vinegar
¼ teaspoon pepper

1. Beat egg slightly in large bowl.
2. Blend in cereal, onion, dry milk, catsup, salt, and pepper.
3. Mix in ground beef.
4. Shape by tablespoonfuls into meatballs.
5. Place in greased, shallow baking pan large enough to keep in single layer.
6. Bake at 400°F. about 12 minutes, until browned.
7. Combine sauce ingredients in large saucepan. Cover and cook over low heat about 15 minutes, stirring often.
8. Put baked meatballs into sauce. Heat about 10 minutes over low heat. Serves 6. Can be served over rice.

Being an example is a full-time job.   RUTH PEALE

SWEDISH MEATBALLS WITH NOODLES

½ cup POST GRAPE-NUTS brand cereal
½ cup water
1 pound ground beef
1 slightly beaten egg
¼ cup chopped onion
1½ teaspoons salt
½ teaspoon nutmeg
2 tablespoons oil
1 can condensed cream of
  celery soup
½ cup water
⅓ cup sour cream
  hot, cooked noodles

1. Mix cereal and ½ cup water. Allow to stand about 1 minute.
2. Add ground beef, egg, onion, salt, and nutmeg.
3. Form into 1-inch balls. Brown in oil in large skillet. Drain excess liquid.
4. Mix soup and ½ cup water. Pour over meatballs. Cover and simmer over low heat 15 minutes.
5. Remove from heat. Add sour cream and stir well.
6. Put hot, cooked noodles in serving dish and cover with meatball mixture. Serves 6.

SLOPPY JOE HAMBURGERS

½ cup POST GRAPE-NUTS brand cereal
½ cup water
1 pound ground beef
¾ teaspoon salt
½ cup chopped onion
1 eight-ounce can tomato sauce
½ cup barbecue sauce
⅛ teaspoon pepper
6 toasted, split hamburger
  buns, buttered

1. Mix cereal and water in large bowl. Let stand about 1 minute.
2. Stir in ground beef. Add salt.
3. Brown onion and the meat mixture in large skillet. Stir in sauces and pepper and heat well.
4. Serve on hamburger buns. Serves 6.

MEATBALLS AND RICE

- 2 cups cornflakes
- 1 pound ground beef
- 1 envelope bleu cheese salad dressing mix
- ½ cup milk
- 2 tablespoons shortening
- ½ cup water
- 1 can condensed tomato soup
- 1 can condensed cream of mushroom soup
- 3 cups fluffy cooked rice

1. Crush cereal a little. Mix with ground beef, salad dressing mix, and milk. Form into small balls.
2. Melt shortening in large skillet. Brown meatballs, turning them frequently. Remove meatballs when browned well.
3. Put water in skillet, bring to boil, and then add soups and stir. Put meatballs back in skillet.
4. Cover and cook on low heat about 5 minutes. Serve over rice, prepared from precooked or regular rice. Serves 6.

We thank Thee, heavenly Father
For every earthly good,
For life, and health, and clothing,
And for our daily food.

CHEESEBURGERS

- 1 slightly beaten egg
- 1 teaspoon seasoned salt
- 1 teaspoon onion powder
- ¼ teaspoon pepper
- 2 teaspoons Worcestershire sauce
- 2 tablespoons milk
- 2 teaspoons snipped parsley
- ¾ cup shredded process cheddar cheese
- 1½ cups CORN CHEX cereal, crushed to ½ cup
- 1 pound lean ground beef

1. Mix egg, salt, onion powder, pepper, Worcestershire sauce, milk, and parsley in large bowl.
2. Stir in shredded cheese, cereal, and meat.
3. Form into 4 patties. Broil 5 to 8 minutes on each side. Serves 4.

He who helps a child helps humanity with an immediateness which no other help given to human creatures in any other stage of human life can possibly give again.   PHILLIPS BROOKS

BEEF PATTIES IN MUSHROOM SAUCE

  ½ cup POST GRAPE-NUTS brand cereal
  ½ cup water
  1 pound ground beef
  ⅓ cup chopped onion
  ½ teaspoon salt
  ⅛ teaspoon pepper
  1 tablespoon oil
  1 can condensed cream
    of mushroom soup
  ½ cup water

1. Mix cereal and ½ cup water in medium-size bowl. Let stand 1 minute.
2. Add ground beef, onion, salt, and pepper.
3. Form mixture into 6 patties.
4. Place oil in heated skillet. Brown patties.
5. Add soup and water. Simmer a few minutes until thoroughly cooked. Serves 6.

BEEF CUTLETS

  1½ cups KELLOGG'S RICE KRISPIES cereal
  1½ pounds ground beef
  ¼ cup chili sauce
  1 slightly beaten egg
  1 teaspoon salt
  1 teaspoon Worcestershire sauce
  2 teaspoons prepared mustard
  3 tablespoons grated onion

1. Crush cereal. Combine rest of ingredients and mix with cereal.
2. Shape into 6 cutlets and place on cookie sheet. Chill. Broil about 8 minutes. Turn and broil 5 minutes. Serves 6.

Add to the pleasure of others.
Subtract from another's unhappiness.
Multiply the pleasures of others.
Divide the good things that come your way.

HAMBURGER STROGANOFF

  ½ cup POST GRAPE-NUTS brand cereal
  ½ cup water
  1 pound ground beef
  1 teaspoon salt
  ⅛ teaspoon pepper
  ½ cup finely chopped onion
  2 four-ounce cans sliced mushrooms,
    drained, or ½ pound fresh mushrooms
  ¾ teaspoon Worcestershire sauce
  6 servings rice
  1 cup sour cream

1. Mix cereal and water in large bowl.
   Let stand 1 minute.
2. Add meat, salt, and pepper. Mix well.
3. Brown well in hot skillet, keeping meat
   in small pieces.
4. Add onion and mushrooms.
   Cook until lightly browned.
5. Add sauce. Simmer 2 minutes.
6. Prepare quick-cooking or regular rice
   according to package directions.
7. Add sour cream to meat mixture.
   Heat but do not boil.
8. Serve meat mixture over rice.
   Serves 6.

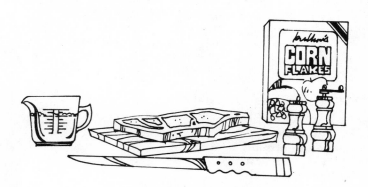

BEEF-AND-RICE PIE

1½ cups **KELLOGG'S PRODUCT 19** cereal, crushed to measure ¾ cup
½ cup milk
¼ cup chopped onion
1 teaspoon salt
1 pound ground beef
1 fifteen-ounce can tomato sauce
1 cup uncooked instant rice
2 tablespoons finely chopped green pepper
¼ teaspoon chili powder
½ cup shredded American cheese

1. Combine cereal, milk, onion, and salt in large bowl. Add ground beef. Mix well.
2. Press into 9-inch pie pan to form pie shell.
3. Combine tomato sauce, rice, pepper, and chili powder in medium-size bowl. Stir well and put into meat pie shell.
4. Bake at 350°F. about 30 minutes, until meat is well cooked. Sprinkle with cheese and bake about 3 minutes longer.
5. Cut into pie-shaped wedges. Serves 6.

With God at our table, we not only ask a blessing, but we have one.
CHARLES H. SPURGEON

MEAT-CRUST PIZZA

½ cup **POST GRAPE-NUTS brand cereal**
½ cup **water**
1 pound **ground beef**
¼ cup **finely chopped onion**
1 **slightly beaten egg**
¾ teaspoon **salt**
¼ teaspoon **garlic salt**
¼ teaspoon **pepper**
1 eight-ounce **can tomato sauce**
⅓ cup **diced green pepper**
¼ teaspoon **oregano**
¼ teaspoon **basil**
¾ cup **grated mozzarella cheese**

1. Mix cereal and water in large bowl. Let stand about 1 minute.
2. Stir in ground beef, onion, egg, salt, garlic salt, and pepper.
3. Press mixture onto greased 12-inch pizza pan, shaping it thickest at the edge.
4. Bake at 400°F. for 15 minutes.
5. Pour tomato sauce over meat. Distribute green pepper, oregano, basil, and cheese over top.
6. Place under broiler about 5 minutes, until cheese melts and browns slightly. Cut in wedges. Serves 6.

PORK STEAK

1½ pounds **pork steak**
1 **egg**
1 cup **crushed cornflakes**
salt and pepper
2 teaspoons **melted butter**
1 cup **hot milk**

1. Dip each steak in slightly beaten egg, then in mixture of cereal, salt, and pepper. Place in baking dish.
2. Pour melted butter over top.
3. Brown at 400°F. Add hot milk. Bake at 350°F. for about 45 minutes, until meat is well done. Serves 4.

SKILLET SUPPER

1½ cups **KELLOGG'S PRODUCT 19 cereal, crushed
to measure ¾ cup**
¼ **cup chopped onion**
1 **teaspoon salt**
⅛ **teaspoon pepper**
1 **tablespoon Worcestershire sauce**
⅓ **cup milk**
1 **pound ground beef**
1 **can tomato soup**
1 **one-pound can pork and beans**
½ **teaspoon chili powder**
½ **cup shredded American cheese**

1. Combine cereal, onion, salt, pepper, Worcestershire
sauce, and milk in large bowl.
2. Add ground beef. Mix well.
3. Form six patties. Brown over medium heat
in large skillet. Drain.
4. Add soup, pork and beans, and chili powder. Stir
carefully. Cover and cook about 30 minutes over low heat,
stirring occasionally.
5. Sprinkle with cheese and cook uncovered 1 or 2 minutes,
until cheese melts. Serve in soup bowls. Serves 6.

---

*We are apt to forget that children watch examples better than they
listen to preaching.*   ROY L. SMITH

HAMBURGER-MASHED POTATO CASSEROLE

½ cup POST GRAPE-NUTS brand cereal
½ cup water
1 pound ground beef
1½ teaspoons salt
⅛ teaspoon pepper
⅛ teaspoon oregano
½ cup chopped onion
2 tablespoons oil
1 sixteen-ounce can stewed tomatoes
3 cups mashed potatoes

1. Mix cereal and water in large bowl. Let stand together about 1 minute.
2. Stir in ground beef, salt, pepper, and oregano.
3. Brown onion and beef mixture in hot oil in large skillet.
4. Drain juice from tomatoes. Stir tomatoes into beef mixture. Put in 9-inch round baking dish. Arrange mashed potatoes on top.
5. Bake at 400°F. for about 30 minutes, until potatoes are light brown. Serves 6.

SCALLOPED CORN AND SAUSAGE

2 eggs
1 cup milk
1 tablespoon all-purpose flour
1 sixteen-ounce can cream-style corn
1 four-ounce can chopped mushrooms, drained
3 cups CORN CHEX cereal, crushed to 1½ cups
1 eight-ounce package brown-and-serve sausage links

1. Beat together in large bowl the eggs, milk, and flour.
2. Stir in corn, mushrooms, and 1 cup of the crushed cereal.
3. Pour into ungreased 8-inch, round baking dish.
4. Arrange sausage links on top, as spokes of a wheel.
5. Sprinkle rest of crushed cereal over top.
6. Bake at 350°F. for 40 to 45 minutes. Serves 6.

CHILI-STUFFED PEPPERS

  6 **large green peppers**
    salt
  1 **pound ground beef**
  1 **medium onion, sliced**
2½ **cups KELLOGG'S RICE KRISPIES cereal**
 ⅛ **teaspoon instant minced**
    garlic
  2 **teaspoons chili powder**
  1 **teaspoon salt**
 ⅛ **teaspoon pepper**
  1 **teaspoon sugar**
 ½ **cup sliced, pitted, ripe olives**
  1 **six-ounce can tomato paste**
  1 **sixteen-ounce can tomatoes, drained**
 ½ **cup grated sharp cheddar cheese**

1. Slice off tops of washed peppers and remove seed core. Sprinkle salt lightly in each and place in 8 x 8 x 2 inch baking dish, hollow side up.
2. Brown ground beef and onion in hot oil until meat loses red color.
3. Add remaining ingredients, except cheese, to the beef mixture. Spoon into peppers.
4. Cover baking dish with foil and bake at 375°F. for 50 minutes or until peppers are tender.
5. Top peppers with cheese and return to oven for 5 minutes or until cheese melts. Serves 6.

Men who won't read the Bible will read "living epistles."

STUFFED PEPPERS

6 medium green peppers
boiling, salted water
½ cup POST GRAPE-NUTS brand cereal
½ cup water
1 pound ground beef
1 eight-ounce can stewed tomatoes
1 teaspoon salt
⅛ teaspoon pepper
½ cup shredded cheddar cheese

1. Remove slice from the top and seeds from inside each pepper.
2. Cook peppers in boiling, salted water about 5 to 10 minutes. Remove from water and drain.
3. Mix cereal and ½ cup water in large bowl. Let stand together about 1 minute.
4. Mix ground beef with soaked cereal. Brown in large skillet. Remove from heat. Drain off excess grease.
5. Add tomatoes, salt, and pepper, and stir.
6. Stuff peppers with mixture. Sprinkle with cheese. Place in shallow baking dish. Bake at 375°F. about 25 minutes. Serves 6.

BAKED FRANKFURTERS

10 frankfurters
½ cup catsup
2 cups cornflakes, crushed
into ½ cup crumbs

1. Dip frankfurters in catsup.
2. Roll in cereal.
3. Put in greased or foil-lined, shallow pan.
4. Bake at 400°F. about 12 minutes, until hot and crisp.
5. Serve with catsup or mustard, if desired. Serves 5.
   Variation: Substitute ½ cup mustard or mixture of ¼ cup catsup and ¼ cup mustard for the catsup in step 1.

We believe that faith and humor go together, that laughing and good times are important for a balanced Christian home.

ARVELLA SCHULLER

BEEF 'N GRANOLA CABBAGE ROLLS

12 large cabbage leaves
1 beaten egg
½ cup water
1 cup granola
¼ cup chopped onion
1 teaspoon salt
¼ teaspoon pepper
¼ teaspoon thyme
1 pound ground beef
1 fifteen-ounce can tomato sauce
2 tablespoons brown sugar
2 tablespoons lemon juice

1. Cover cabbage leaves with boiling water for about 3 minutes, until limp. Drain.
2. Mix beaten egg and ½ cup water. Add cereal, onion, salt, pepper, and thyme. Stir in ground beef.
3. Put about ¼ cup meat mixture on each cabbage leaf. Fold in sides and roll ends over top. Fasten with toothpicks. Put in a large skillet.
4. Mix tomato sauce, sugar, and lemon juice. Pour over cabbage rolls. Cover and simmer about 1 hour. Baste occasionally. Remove cover and cook about 5 minutes more, until sauce has thickened slightly. Serves 6.

A pint of example is worth a gallon of advice.

TUNA-RICE CASSEROLE

1 seven-ounce can tuna
½ cup uncooked rice
1 can cream of mushroom soup
1 can cream of chicken soup
1 cup cooked peas
½ cup crushed cornflakes

1. Drain tuna.
2. Combine tuna, rice, soups, and peas. Place in baking dish.
3. Top with crushed cereal. Bake at 350°F. about 1 hour.

GERMAN-STYLE CABBAGE ROLLS

1 medium cabbage
½ cup POST GRAPE-NUTS brand cereal
½ cup water
1 pound ground beef
1 cup chopped onion
1½ teaspoons salt
½ teaspoon garlic salt
⅛ teaspoon pepper
1 tablespoon oil
½ teaspoon caraway seed
1 beef bouillon cube
½ cup boiling water

1. Cook cabbage in boiling, salted water for 6 to 8 minutes. Drain and pull off six outside leaves.
2. Chop rest of cabbage coarsely and put aside.
3. Mix cereal with ½ cup water. Let stand 1 or 2 minutes.
4. Blend ground beef, ½ cup chopped onion, 1 teaspoon salt, the garlic salt, and pepper with softened cereal.
5. Divide meat mixture into 6 parts and spoon onto cabbage leaves. Roll up, tuck ends under, and fasten with toothpicks if needed.
6. Place stuffed leaves in large, shallow casserole.
7. In heavy skillet, brown remaining onion and chopped cabbage. When tender, stir in caraway seed and the ½ teaspoon salt. Spread over cabbage rolls.
8. Dissolve bouillon cube in the ½ cup boiling water and pour over cabbage.
9. Cover casserole and bake at 350°F. for about 1 hour. Serves 6.

BEEF-VEGETABLE CASSEROLE

½ cup POST GRAPE-NUTS brand cereal
½ cup water
1 pound ground beef
2 teaspoons salt
½ teaspoon pepper
2 coarsely chopped onions
1 cup thinly sliced carrots
3 cups thinly sliced potatoes
1 sixteen-ounce can stewed tomatoes

1. Mix cereal and water in large bowl. Let stand about 1 minute.
2. Add meat, 1 teaspoon of the salt, and ¼ teaspoon of the pepper. Brown mixture in skillet. Put in 2 quart baking dish.
3. Cover with chopped onion, carrot slices, and potato slices in layers. Sprinkle with the other teaspoon of salt and ¼ teaspoon of pepper.
4. Pour tomatoes over top. Cover. Bake at 350°F. for 1 hour. Uncover and bake another 30 minutes. Serves 8.

Praise to God, the Father good,
For daily grace, for daily food;
For sun and rain, for harvest blest,
For promise of eternal rest.

SALMON PATTIES

2 eggs
1 cup finely crushed cornflakes
1 fifteen-and-a-half-ounce can salmon
½ teaspoon salt
⅛ teaspoon pepper
2 tablespoons dried parsley flakes
3 tablespoons finely chopped onion
¼ cup milk
vegetable oil

1. Beat egg slightly in medium-size bowl. Add ½ cup of the cereal crumbs, salmon, salt, pepper, parsley flakes, onion, and milk.
2. Mix well. Shape into 12 patties, about 2½ inches across. Coat with rest of cereal.
3. Fry in small amount of oil in large skillet about 2 minutes on each side, until browned. Serves 6.

SKILLET DINNER

   2 **nine-ounce packages frozen,
      French-style green beans**
   ½ **cup POST GRAPE-NUTS brand cereal**
   ½ **cup water**
   1 **pound ground beef**
   ½ **cup chopped onion**
   1 **tablespoon oil**
   1 **can cream of mushroom
      or tomato soup**
   1 **cup water**
   1 **teaspoon salt**

1. Cook beans as directed on package.
2. Mix cereal and ½ cup water and allow to stand for 1 minute.
3. Stir in ground beef and chopped onion.
4. Brown in oil in hot skillet.
5. When meat mixture is browned, add soup, 1 cup water, salt, and cooked beans. Heat well. Serves 6.

Jesus was indignant when the disciples thought children were not of sufficient importance to occupy his attention. Compared with the selfish ambition of grown-ups he felt something heavenly in children, a breath of the Kingdom of God....To inflict any spiritual injury on one of these little ones seemed to him an inexpressible guilt.

WALTER RAUSCHENBUSCH

CRUNCHY PORK CHOPS

   ¾ **cup crushed POST GRAPE-NUTS brand cereal**
   1 **teaspoon garlic salt**
   ½ **teaspoon salt**
   8 **pork chops**

1. Mix crushed cereal, garlic salt, and salt together.
2. Moisten chops with water. Dip both sides in cereal mixture.
3. Put on rack in baking pan. Bake at 400°F. for 40 to 50 minutes, until thoroughly cooked. Serves 8.

CHILI

½ cup POST GRAPE-NUTS brand cereal
½ cup water
1 pound ground beef
½ cup chopped onion
¼ cup chopped green pepper
1 sixteen-ounce can tomatoes
1 fifteen-ounce can red kidney
  beans, drained
1 eight-ounce can tomato sauce
1 tablespoon chili powder
1 teaspoon salt
  dash of pepper

1. Mix cereal and water in large saucepan. Let stand 1 minute.
2. Add ground beef. Stir. Brown with onion and green pepper.
3. Add remaining ingredients. Bring to boil. Cover and simmer about 45 minutes, stirring as needed. Serves 4 to 6.

No man can sincerely try to help another without helping himself.

J. B. WEBSTER

HAM LOAF

3 eggs
¾ cup finely crushed cornflakes
¼ cup firmly packed brown sugar
½ cup milk
⅓ cup finely chopped onion
½ teaspoon salt
⅛ teaspoon pepper
1½ teaspoons dry mustard
1½ pounds ground, cooked ham
½ pound ground pork

1. Beat eggs slightly in large bowl.
2. Add cereal, brown sugar, milk, onion, salt, pepper, and mustard. Mix well.
3. Mix in the meats. Shape and put in greased loaf pan.
4. Bake at 350°F. about 75 minutes. Serves 10 to 12.

BAKED HASH

- 1½ cups coarsely ground, cooked beef
- 1 cup coarsely ground, cooked potatoes
- ½ cup coarsely ground onion
- ¼ cup chopped parsley
- 1 teaspoon salt
  dash of pepper
- 2 teaspoons Worcestershire sauce
- 1 five-and-a-third-ounce can (⅔ cup) evaporated milk

TOPPING

- ⅓ cup slightly crushed cornflakes
- 1 tablespoon melted margarine

1. Stir meat, potatoes, onion, parsley, salt, pepper, Worcestershire sauce, and milk together in large bowl.
2. Put in greased 1 quart baking dish.
3. Combine cereal and margarine. Sprinkle over top.
4. Bake at 350°F. for 30 minutes. Serve with catsup. Serves 4.

What I kept, I lost.
What I spent, I had.
What I gave, I have.

PERSIAN PROVERB

CRISP OVEN-FRIED CHICKEN

- ¾ cup margarine
- 1¼ teaspoons Italian dressing
- ¾ teaspoon salt
- 1 tablespoon minced onion
- ⅛ teaspoon pepper
- ½ cup all-purpose flour
  about 2½ pounds chicken parts
- 5 cups CORN CHEX cereal, crushed to 1⅔ cups

1. Melt margarine in small pan. Add seasonings and flour. Mix well.
2. Dip chicken pieces in margarine and flour mixture, then roll in crushed cereal. Dry on rack about 15 minutes.
3. Place in shallow baking dish. Bake at 375°F. for 60 to 90 minutes. Serves 4 to 6.

BEEF-STUFFED ZUCCHINI

½ cup **POST GRAPE-NUTS**
 brand cereal
½ cup water
1 pound ground beef
6 small zucchini, halved
 lengthwise
 salt and pepper
½ cup chopped onion
2 tablespoons oil
3 tablespoons chopped
 parsley
2 tablespoons catsup
1 teaspoon salt
 dash of pepper
½ cup grated Parmesan or
 cheddar cheese

1. Mix cereal and water in medium-size bowl.
 Let stand 1 minute.
2. Add ground beef and stir.
3. Remove and chop centers from zucchini. Sprinkle
 shells lightly with salt and pepper.
4. Sauté chopped zucchini and onion in oil in skillet until
 tender. Combine with meat and cereal mixture. Add
 parsley, catsup, salt, and pepper.
5. Spoon into zucchini shells. Bake at 350°F. for about 35
 minutes. Sprinkle with cheese. Bake about 10 minutes
 more, until zucchini is tender. Serves 6.

Train up a child in the way he should go,
Even when he is old he will not depart from it.   PROVERBS 22:6

SPAGHETTI SAUCE

½ cup **POST GRAPE-NUTS** brand cereal
½ cup water
1 pound ground beef
½ cup chopped onion
¼ cup chopped green pepper
1 clove garlic, minced
1 tablespoon oil
1 twenty-eight ounce can
  whole tomatoes
1 six-ounce can tomato paste
2 teaspoons salt
1 teaspoon sugar
1 bay leaf
⅛ teaspoon pepper
¼ teaspoon thyme
1 teaspoon oregano
1 cup water

1. Pour ½ cup water over cereal. Let stand 1 or 2 minutes.
2. Stir in ground beef, onion, green pepper, and garlic. Brown in hot oil in large skillet.
3. Drain off excess fat. Add tomatoes, tomato paste, salt, sugar, bay leaf and other seasonings, and 1 cup water.
4. Bring to boil, reduce heat, cover, and simmer 1 hour. Stir occasionally. Serves 6 to 8.

CHICKEN BAKED IN CORNFLAKES

1 cup crushed cornflakes
1 teaspoon salt
¼ teaspoon pepper
1 two-and-a-half- to three-pound frying
  chicken, cut into serving pieces
½ cup evaporated milk

1. Combine crushed cereal, salt, and pepper in a shallow dish.
2. Put evaporated milk in another shallow dish.
3. Dip chicken pieces first in milk, then roll in seasoned cereal crumbs.
4. Place in shallow baking pan, skin side up. Bake at 350°F. about 1 hour.

HAWAIIAN-STYLE CHICKEN

> 3 **pounds chicken pieces, washed and dried**
> 1 **teaspoon salt**
> 1 **slightly beaten egg**
> ⅓ **cup frozen pineapple-orange juice concentrate, thawed**
> 1 **cup finely crushed cornflakes**
> ½ **cup shredded coconut**
> ½ **teaspoon curry powder**
> 3 **tablespoons melted margarine**

1. Spread chicken pieces out in shallow pan. Sprinkle salt over them.
2. Combine egg and juice. Pour over chicken. Cover and chill for 1 hour or more, turning pieces of chicken occasionally.
3. In shallow dish, combine cereal, coconut, and curry powder.
4. Drain excess moisture from chicken pieces. Dip into cereal mixture. Place skin sides up in greased, shallow baking pan. Drizzle with melted margarine.
5. Bake uncovered at 375°F. about 1 hour, until tender. Garnish with pineapple or orange slices. Serves 6.
   Variation: Dilute balance of pineapple-orange juice concentrate according to package directions. Use as liquid in which to cook rice to serve with chicken.

An ounce of practice is worth a pound of preach.

CHICKEN BAKED WITH MUSHROOM SOUP

1 can cream of mushroom soup
¾ cup milk
¼ teaspoon poultry seasoning
1½ cups crushed cornflakes
2 tablespoons toasted sesame seeds
2 pounds chicken parts
2 tablespoons melted margarine

1. Combine ¼ cup soup, ¼ cup milk, and ⅛ teaspoon poultry seasoning in shallow dish.
2. Combine crushed cereal and sesame seeds in another shallow dish.
3. Dip chicken pieces in soup mixture and then roll in cereal.
4. Put chicken pieces in shallow baking dish. Drizzle with margarine.
5. Bake at 400°F. for ½ hour. Reduce temperature to 350°F. and continue baking another 30 to 40 minutes.
6. Combine and heat together rest of soup, milk, and poultry seasoning. Pour over chicken when ready to serve. Serves 4.

GRAPE-NUTTY CHICKEN

1 cup POST GRAPE-NUTS brand cereal
1 teaspoon salt
½ teaspoon garlic salt
⅛ teaspoon pepper
2 tablespoons salad oil
2½ pounds frying chicken pieces

1. Crush cereal into fine crumbs. Combine with seasonings. Sprinkle salad oil over seasoned crumbs. Stir with fork.
2. Dip chicken pieces in water, then in cereal mixture.
3. Put in ungreased, shallow pan. Bake at 400°F. for 40 to 60 minutes, until chicken is well done. Serves 4 to 6.

"Helping God bloom His roses" is *work fit for a king, a king "whose strength is as the strength of ten because his heart is pure." It will make him more than a king — it will make him kingly!*

DANIEL A. POLING

PARTY CHICKEN CASSEROLE

1 can cream of chicken soup
¾ cup mayonnaise
1 teaspoon finely chopped onion
1 teaspoon salt
1 teaspoon lemon juice
3 cups diced, cooked chicken
¼ cup chicken broth
1 cup finely cut celery
1 cup cooked rice
1 cup drained, sliced water chestnuts
3 hard-cooked eggs, coarsely chopped
¼ cup melted margarine
1 cup crushed cornflakes
½ cup slivered almonds

1. Blend soup, mayonnaise, onion, salt, and lemon juice until smooth.
2. Combine chicken pieces, broth, celery, rice, water chestnuts, and hard-cooked eggs in shallow baking dish. Cover with sauce.
3. Combine melted margarine, crushed cereal, and slivered almonds. Sprinkle over top of casserole.
4. Bake at 350°F. for 30 minutes. Add some chicken broth during baking if mixture appears too dry. Serves 6 to 8.

We talk about God being a helper, friend, and Savior, but a child and an adult need to hear that God is their helper, their friend, and their personal Savior.   EVELYN ROBERTS

CHICKEN-NOODLE CASSEROLE

1 can cream of mushroom soup
½ cup milk
1 to 1½ cups cooked or canned,
**   diced chicken**
2 cups cooked medium noodles
½ cup cooked green beans
2 tablespoons slightly crushed cornflakes

1. Combine soup and milk in 1½ quart casserole.
2. Add diced chicken, cooked noodles, and cooked green beans. Mix well.
3. Top with crushed cereal.
4. Bake at 350°F. for 30 minutes. Serves 4.
Variation: Omit green beans if preferred. Turkey may be substituted for chicken.

CHICKEN BAKED IN RICE KRISPIES

½ cup margarine
1 teaspoon salt
¼ teaspoon pepper
1 cup crushed KELLOGG'S RICE
**   KRISPIES cereal**
1 fryer, cut into pieces

1. Melt margarine. Add salt and pepper.
2. Put crushed cereal into shallow bowl.
3. Dip chicken pieces into margarine, then coat with cereal.
4. Place in shallow baking pan. Bake at 350°F. about 1 hour.

Our children are unique. we recognize they're different and have different needs....Our goal is to love each child in a very special way, as a very special person, created by God himself!

ALICE SCHRAGE

TURKEY CASSEROLE

3 cups RICE CHEX cereal,
  crushed to 1½ cups
2 tablespoons melted margarine
⅛ teaspoon and ⅛ teaspoon
  ground oregano
2 tablespoons grated Parmesan cheese
1 ten-and-three-quarter-ounce can
  cream of mushroom soup
1½ cups evaporated milk
¼ teaspoon onion powder
1¼ teaspoons seasoned salt
1 teaspoon dried parsley flakes
3 cups chopped, cooked turkey
⅓ cup chopped, ripe olives
6 lasagna noodles, cooked according
  to package directions
⅔ cup shredded mozzarella cheese

1. Mix cereal, margarine, ⅛ teaspoon oregano, and Parmesan cheese.
2. Mix soup, milk, onion powder, salt, parsley flakes, and ⅛ teaspoon oregano. Add turkey and olives, and mix well.
3. Grease 13 x 9 x 2 inch baking dish. Put 3 lasagna noodles across bottom, then half the soup mixture. Repeat and top with cereal mixture.
4. Bake at 375°F. about 30 minutes, until bubbly around edges. Cool slightly. Cut into 6 squares for large servings or more for smaller servings.

Let love, genuine love, pervade our conversations. Let laughter give it joy and flavor.   MARJORIE HOLMES

SALMON AND EGGS AU GRATIN

3 tablespoons margarine
4 tablespoons flour
2 cups milk
1 teaspoon salt
⅛ teaspoon pepper
2 cups canned salmon
1 tablespoon lemon juice
2 hard-cooked eggs, sliced
1 cup crushed cornflakes
½ cup grated American cheese

1. Melt margarine in saucepan. Add flour and mix well.
2. Add milk, salt, and pepper, cooking and stirring
   until thick, white sauce is formed.
3. Flake salmon after removing skin and bones. Place flaked
   salmon in 2½ quart baking dish. Sprinkle with lemon
   juice. Spread sliced eggs, ½ cup crushed cereal, and
   ¼ cup grated cheese on top.
4. Cover with white sauce. Sprinkle with rest of cornflakes
   and cheese. Bake uncovered at 375°F. for 25 minutes.
   Serves 6.

DOUBLE-COATED CHICKEN

1 egg
1 cup milk
1 cup all-purpose flour
1½ teaspoons salt
¼ teaspoon pepper
3 pounds frying chicken pieces,
   washed and patted dry
1¾ cups finely crushed cornflakes
3 tablespoons melted margarine

1. Beat egg and milk slightly in medium-size bowl.
2. Add flour, salt, and pepper. Beat until smooth.
3. Dip chicken pieces in batter. Roll in cereal crumbs.
4. Place in greased or foil-lined baking pan. Drizzle each
   piece of chicken with melted margarine.
5. Bake uncovered at 350°F. about 1 to 1½ hours, until
   chicken is tender. Serves 6.

BAKED SALMON

⅓ cup dairy sour cream
½ cup milk
3 eggs, separated
2 cups KELLOGG'S RICE KRISPIES cereal
1 fifteen-and-a-half-ounce can (2 cups) salmon, drained, skinned, boned, and flaked
¼ cup finely chopped onion
¼ cup chopped celery
1 tablespoon dried parsley flakes
1 tablespoon lemon juice
½ teaspoon salt
⅛ teaspoon pepper
1 cup mayonnaise
1 tablespoon prepared mustard

1. Mix sour cream, milk, and egg yolks in large bowl. Beat well. Add cereal and stir. Let stand about 5 minutes. Beat well.
2. Add salmon, onion, celery, 2 teaspoons of parsley flakes, lemon juice, salt, and pepper to cereal mixture. Stir well.
3. Beat 2 egg whites in small bowl until stiff but not dry. Fold into salmon mixture.
4. Spoon into greased 1½ quart baking dish. Bake at 375°F. about 30 minutes, until knife comes out clean.
5. Mix mayonnaise and mustard in small bowl. Beat rest of egg white in a clean, small bowl, until stiff but not dry. Fold into mayonnaise and mustard mixture. When salmon dish is baked, spread mayonnaise mixture over top. Return to oven and bake another 5 minutes.
6. After removing from oven, sprinkle rest of parsley flakes over top. Serve hot. Serves 6.

Make others happy, and you will be happy yourself.

CRISPY FISH CASSEROLE

2 egg yolks
2 cups milk
2 tablespoons quick-cooking tapioca
1 teaspoon salt
  dash of pepper
½ cup finely chopped celery
1½ teaspoons grated onion
2 cups flaked, cooked fish
2 tablespoons chopped parsley
2 egg whites
½ cup crushed cornflakes

1. Combine egg yolks and a little milk in medium-size saucepan.
2. Add rest of milk, tapioca, salt, pepper, celery, and onion. Stirring constantly, bring mixture to a boil over medium heat.
3. Remove from heat. Stir in fish and parsley.
4. Beat egg whites until stiff. Gradually fold milk mixture into egg whites.
5. Spoon into greased 1½ quart baking dish. Top with crushed cornflakes. Bake at 350°F. for about 50 minutes. Serves 4 to 6.

What is a family meant to be? Among other things, I personally have always felt it is meant to be a museum of memories — *collections of carefully preserved memories and a realization that day-by-day memories are being chosen for our museum. Someone in the family — one who is happily making it his or her career, or both parents, perhaps a grandparent or two, aunts and uncles, older brothers and sisters — at least one person needs to be conscious that memories are important, and that time can be made to have double value by recognizing that what is done today will be tomorrow's memory.*   EDITH SCHAEFFER

SALMON BALLS

1½ cups finely crushed cornflakes
1 fifteen-and-a-half-ounce can salmon, drained, skinned, boned, and flaked
1 cup evaporated milk
¼ cup pickle relish
¼ cup finely chopped celery
2 tablespoons finely chopped onion
2 tablespoons melted margarine

1. Combine half the crushed cereal, the salmon, ½ cup of the milk, the relish, celery, and onion.
2. Shape into 10 or 12 balls. Dip in rest of milk. Coat with rest of cereal. Put in shallow baking pan, leaving a little space between them.
3. Drizzle melted margarine on each salmon ball. Bake at 350°F. about 35 minutes, until light brown. Serves 5 or 6.

No child is ready for life until he for himself had adopted the right standards and ideals, and they have become his very own.
ELIZABETH WALKER STRACHAN

TUNA-NOODLE CASSEROLE

1 ten-ounce package frozen mixed vegetables
1 can cream of mushroom soup
¾ cup milk
1 seven-ounce can tuna, drained and flaked
1 cup grated cheddar cheese
4 ounces egg noodles, cooked and drained
2 tablespoons finely chopped onion
½ teaspoon prepared mustard
¼ teaspoon salt
2 cups POST GRAPE-NUTS FLAKES
2 tablespoons melted margarine

1. Combine vegetables, soup, and milk in heavy saucepan. Bring to boil in large saucepan, stirring to mix well.
2. Remove from heat. Add drained tuna, grated cheese, cooked noodles, onion, mustard, and salt. Stir carefully.
3. Pour into 2½ quart baking dish. Bake at 400°F. about 15 minutes, until mixture begins to bubble.
4. Mix cereal and margarine. Sprinkle over top of casserole. Bake about 5 minutes more, until browned. Serves 6 to 8.

Just as we mix certain foods together for added nourishment, so we must mix faith with each verse that we read. It is written of some listeners that "the word did not profit them, not being mixed with faith by them that heard it" (Hebrews 4:2).   ELSIE D. HOLSINGER

TUNA SALAD

    2 cups CORN CHEX cereal, crushed to 1½ cups
    1 six-and-a-half-ounce can chunk light tuna, drained and flaked
    2 hard-cooked eggs, finely chopped
    1 apple, cored and chopped
   ½ cup chopped celery
   ¼ cup sweet pickle relish
    2 teaspoons finely chopped onion
    1 teaspoon lemon juice
   ⅔ to 1 cup mayonnaise

1. Combine all ingredients, stirring with a light touch.
2. Chill in refrigerator for 1 hour or more before serving.
3. Just before serving, put salad on lettuce leaves. Serves 6.

CRISPY BAKED FISH

> 1 **pound fish fillets or steak**
> ¼ **cup melted butter or margarine**
> 1 **cup finely crushed cornflakes**
> ½ **teaspoon salt**
> ¼ **teaspoon pepper**
> ⅓ **cup evaporated milk**

1. Cut fish into serving portions.
2. Cover bottom of shallow pan with foil, turning it up around the edges.
3. Brush the foil with some of the melted butter.
4. Combine cereal crumbs, salt, and pepper in a shallow bowl.
5. Dip each piece of fish in evaporated milk and then in seasoned cereal.
6. Arrange on foil. Pour remaining butter over fish. Bake at 375°F. about 20 to 30 minutes, until crisp. Serves 4.

We thank Thee for our homes and friends,
For food and shelter, too.
May we be always kind and good,
And to the Lord be true.
AMEN

BAKED FISH FILLETS

> 2 **pounds fish fillets**
> 3 **cups KELLOGG'S RICE KRISPIES cereal,**
>   **crushed to measure 1½ cups**
> ½ **teaspoon salt**
> ⅛ **teaspoon pepper**
> 1 **tablespoon dried parsley flakes**
> ½ **cup butter**

1. Dry fish with paper towels.
2. Combine crushed cereal, salt, pepper, and parsley in shallow bowl.
3. Melt butter. Dip fish fillets in butter and then coat with cereal.
4. Place in greased, shallow baking pan.
5. Bake uncovered at 375°F. about 25 minutes. Serves 6 to 8.

CLAM PATTIES

   ¼ **cup all-purpose flour**
   ½ **teaspoon baking powder**
   ¼ **teaspoon salt**
   ⅛ **teaspoon black pepper**
   1 **tablespoon snipped parsley**
   1 **six-and-a-half-ounce can minced**
     clams, drained (reserve liquid)
   1 **beaten egg**
   2 **cups RICE CHEX cereal**

1. Mix together flour, baking powder, salt, pepper, and parsley.
2. Add liquid from clams. Stir until smooth.
3. Mix in beaten egg and clams.
4. Add cereal. Stir lightly. Let stand 10 minutes and stir again.
5. Heat oil to depth of about ⅛ inch in large skillet.
6. Drop clam mixture into hot oil by heaping tablespoonfuls. Shape with wooden spoon into patties.
7. Turning once, brown both sides over medium heat.
8. Place briefly on paper towels to absorb excess grease. Serve hot. Makes 8 patties.

We have not learned to look on youth with Christian eyes until we see in them God's coming servants, the living promises of a new day and a better time.   R. E. O. WHITE

FRIED FISH

   1 **pound of fish**
   1 **beaten egg**
   1 **cup finely crushed cornflakes**
     vegetable oil
     salt
     pepper

1. Dip fish in beaten egg, then in cereal.
2. Heat about ¼ inch oil in large, heavy skillet.
3. Fry fish, seasoning with salt and pepper before and after turning.
4. Serve hot. Serves 4.

7
Snacks

KIX MIX

- ¼ **cup margarine**
- 2 **tablespoons salad oil**
- ½ **cup mixed nuts or peanuts**
- 2 **cups pretzels**
- 2 **cups RICE CHEX cereal**
- 2 **cups KIX breakfast cereal**

1. Melt margarine in small saucepan. Blend in oil.
2. Mix nuts, pretzels, and cereals in large bowl.
3. Pour margarine and oil over cereal mixture. Mix well.
4. Heat at 225°F. about 1½ hours. Makes about 6 cups.

Christ's presence in the carpenter's shop for eighteen years of His life has forever sanctified work. Possibly nothing would be more beneficial to our children in connection with work than to try to get across to them the idea expressed on the little card over the kitchen sink of the bishop's wife: "Divine service will be conducted here three times daily."

ELIZABETH WALKER STRACHAN

CHEESE AND CEREAL SNACK

2 cups RICE CHEX cereal
3 tablespoons melted margarine
¼ cup grated Parmesan cheese

1. Combine cereal and margarine in 8 x 8 x 2 inch pan.
2. Sprinkle grated cheese over cereal.
3. Heat at 300°F. about 15 minutes, stirring a few times. Cool.

CHEX SNACKING MIX

6 tablespoons butter or margarine
1 teaspoon seasoned salt
4 teaspoons Worcestershire sauce
2 cups CORN CHEX cereal
2 cups RICE CHEX cereal
2 cups WHEAT CHEX cereal
1 cup salted mixed nuts

1. Melt butter or margarine in large, shallow baking pan over low heat.
2. Add seasoned salt and Worcestershire sauce.
3. Stir in cereals and nuts. Mix well.
4. Heat in oven at 250°F. about 45 minutes, stirring every 15 minutes.
5. Spread out on paper towels to cool. Makes about 7 cups.
   Variations: Substitute ¼ teaspoon of onion or garlic salt and ½ teaspoon salt for 1 teaspoon seasoned salt.
   Substitute 2½ teaspoons soy sauce for 4 teaspoons Worcestershire sauce.
   Substitute cashews, pecans, or peanuts for mixed nuts.
   Use popcorn, pretzel sticks, or Chinese noodles in place of nuts or some of the cereal.

All the members of Christ have need one of another....Therefore let none despise the least member.   GEORGE FOX

CORNFLAKES SNACK

4 cups cornflakes
1 cup small pretzels
1 cup mixed nuts
2 tablespoons melted butter
2 teaspoons garlic salad dressing mix

1. Spread cereal in large, shallow baking pan.
2. Heat cereal in oven at 300°F. about 5 minutes. Remove from oven, but leave oven on.
3. Carefully stir in pretzels and nuts.
4. Pour melted butter over mixture. Sprinkle with salad dressing mix. Stir until cereal is well coated.
5. Heat another 15 to 20 minutes. Makes 6 cups.

PEANUTTY SNACK

4 cups CHEERIOS breakfast cereal
1 cup dry-roasted peanuts
¼ cup margarine
2 tablespoons peanut butter
¼ teaspoon cinnamon

1. Combine cereal and peanuts in large bowl.
2. In small saucepan, melt margarine and peanut butter over low heat. Stir in cinnamon.
3. Pour liquid mixture over cereal. Mix well.
4. Spread in large, shallow baking pan.
5. Heat at 350°F. for 10 to 12 minutes, stirring after 5 minutes. Makes 5 cups.

The child is fortunate indeed who has in his background memories of satisfying times at Grandma and Grandpa's house.　　BETTY LAND

TASTY WHEAT SNACK

    4 cups bite-size wheat biscuits
    ⅓ cup melted margarine
    1½ teaspoons seasoned salt
    1½ cups pretzel sticks
    ½ cup salted peanuts
    ⅓ cup dark, seedless raisins

1. Spread cereal out on large, shallow pan.
2. Combine melted margarine and seasoned salt in small saucepan. Pour slowly over cereal.
3. Add pretzels and peanuts. Mix together.
4. Bake at 350°F. for 15 minutes. Then add raisins, stirring to mix. Can be served warm or cold. Makes about 6 cups.

GOLDEN GRAHAM MUNCH

    1 twelve-ounce can mixed nuts or
    1 twelve-ounce jar dry-roasted peanuts
    ¼ cup melted margarine
    ¼ cup grated Parmesan cheese
    ¼ teaspoon garlic powder
    ¼ teaspoon ground oregano
    ¼ teaspoon celery salt
    4 cups GOLDEN GRAHAMS breakfast cereal

1. Put nuts into medium-size bowl. Melt margarine.
2. Stir cheese, garlic powder, oregano, and celery salt into melted margarine. Pour over nuts and mix well.
3. Spread out in shallow, ungreased baking pan.
4. Heat at 300°F. for about 15 minutes, stirring occasionally. Add cereal immediately and stir. Cool.
5. Store in tightly covered container. Makes about 6 cups.

For growing children at play, there is nothing so interesting as really 'doing things.' To 'help cook' is one of the most enjoyable things of childhood — to say nothing of being a sure way of producing good cooks.
          EDITH SCHAEFFER

HIKER'S TREAT

1 cup CAP'N CRUNCH
1 cup raisins
1 cup chocolate chips
1 cup salted peanuts

1. Combine all ingredients. Mix well.
2. Package in individual plastic bags for convenient snacking. Makes 4 cups.

FROZEN BANANA-ON-A-STICK

1½ cups KELLOGG'S RICE KRISPIES cereal
3 tablespoons margarine
½ cup chocolate chips
4 firm bananas
8 wooden skewers

1. Put cereal in shallow dish.
2. Melt margarine and chocolate chips together over low heat, stirring until smooth. Pour into another shallow dish.
3. Peel bananas and split each in half crosswise. Insert wooden stick into cut end of each half.
4. Dip each into chocolate mixture. Turn to coat evenly.
5. Roll in cereal and press cereal into chocolate.
6. Place on waxed paper placed on flat tray. Freeze about 2 hours. Serve when frozen or wrap in foil to serve later. Serves 8.

Variations: Use KELLOGG'S COCOA KRISPIES cereal or crushed CORN CHEX cereal in place of KELLOGG'S RICE KRISPIES cereal.

Substitute butterscotch chips for chocolate chips and ¾ cup peanut butter with 2 tablespoons corn oil for 3 tablespoons margarine.

PEANUT BUTTER AND RAISIN SNACK

1 **twelve-ounce package (2 cups)
peanut butter chips**
1 **cup golden, seedless raisins**
1 **cup dark, seedless raisins**
2 **cups GOLDEN GRAHAMS breakfast cereal**
1 **cup miniature marshmallows**

1. Mix peanut butter chips, raisins, cereal, and marshmallows in large bowl.
2. Store in covered plastic container. Use as desired for snacking. Makes about 7 cups.

Duty makes us do things well, but love makes us do them beautifully.
PHILLIPS BROOKS

HONEY-GRANOLA SNACK

⅓ cup melted margarine
⅓ cup firmly packed brown sugar
¼ cup honey
3 cups granola

1. Put margarine, sugar, and honey in saucepan. Stir over low heat until well blended.
2. Put cereal in large bowl. Pour warm mixture over cereal and mix well.
3. Press into foil-lined 9 x 9 x 2 inch pan. Bake at 450°F. about 6 to 8 minutes, until brown and bubbly. Cool. Remove from pan. Cut into small, snack-size pieces. Keep in refrigerator. Makes about 4 cups.

Thank You for the world so sweet,
Thank You for the food we eat,
Thank You for the birds that sing,
Thank You, God, for everything.
AMEN.

CINNAMON-BRAN MUNCH

⅓ cup sugar
1¼ teaspoons cinnamon
4 tablespoons margarine
3 cups BRAN CHEX cereal

1. In small bowl, combine sugar and cinnamon.
2. In large skillet, melt margarine over low heat. Add cereal. Stir carefully until all cereal is coated. Heat and stir gently another 5 minutes.
3. Sprinkle half the sugar mixture over coated cereal. Stir well, bringing cereal from bottom of skillet to top. Sprinkle with rest of sugar mixture. Keep heating and stirring 1 more minute.
4. Cool on paper toweling. Makes 3 cups.

HIGH ENERGY SNACK

2 cups GOLDEN GRAHAMS breakfast cereal
1 cup golden raisins
1 cup dark raisins
1 cup peanuts

1. Combine cereal, raisins, and nuts in large bowl. Mix well.
2. Store in tightly covered container. Makes 5 cups.
   Variations: Any or all of the following ingredients can be added to those listed: cut-up, dried pears; cut-up, dried apricots; chopped walnuts; and chocolate candies or chocolate chips.

There is an old axiom (Emerson said it first, I think) to the effect that "What you are speaks so loud that I cannot hear what you say." If we tell our children not to do something because it is wrong for them to do it, then we should not do it, either. The best teaching is example. Words are easy, deeds are hard, but deeds get the job done.

DALE EVANS ROGERS

GRANOLA SNACK

1 cup granola
1 cup chopped, dried apricots
1 cup salted peanuts
1 cup chocolate chips
1 cup miniature marshmallows

1. Combine ingredients in large bowl.
2. Store well covered. Makes 5 cups.
   Variation: Any 1 or 2 of the last 4 ingredients may be omitted for variety.

BRAN SQUARES

½ cup honey
½ cup peanut butter
3 tablespoons margarine
½ cup nonfat dry milk powder
2½ cups KELLOGG'S ALL-BRAN cereal
3 tablespoons toasted sesame seeds

1. In medium-size saucepan, melt together honey, peanut butter, and margarine, stirring constantly.
2. Remove from heat and add dry milk and cereal. Mix well.
3. Press into 8 x 8 x 2 inch pan. Press sesame seeds into top.
4. Cool. Cut into 16 squares.

An atmosphere of love is the most healthful atmosphere — mentally, physically, and spiritually — in which a child can grow. Love is the sunshine essential for a soul's growth.

ELIZABETH WALKER STRACHAN

GARLIC STICKS

2 cups CORN CHEX cereal, crushed to ¾ cup
½ teaspoon garlic powder
¼ teaspoon salt
2 tablespoons melted margarine
1 eight-ounce package refrigerated biscuits

1. In small bowl, mix crushed cereal, garlic powder, and salt.
2. Pour melted margarine over cereal mixture. Mix well.
3. Put portion of crumbs on sheet of waxed paper.
4. Cut each biscuit in half. Roll in crumbs, shaping into 8-inch-long sticks and letting cereal crumbs work into dough. Add crumbs as needed until all are used. Place sticks on cookie sheets.
5. Bake at 450°F. for 5 to 8 minutes. Serve hot. Makes 20.

TOASTY CHEESE SANDWICHES

>   3 cups KELLOGG'S RICE KRISPIES cereal,
>   crushed to measure 1½ cups
>   4 slices cheese
>   8 slices day-old bread
>   2 eggs
>   ½ cup milk
>   ¼ teaspoon salt
>   3 tablespoons melted margarine

1. Place crushed cereal in shallow dish.
2. Make 4 sandwiches by placing 1 slice cheese between 2 slices of bread for each sandwich.
3. In another shallow dish, beat eggs, milk, and salt until foamy.
4. Dip each sandwich in egg mixture and then in crushed cereal, coating both sides.
5. Place on greased cookie sheet. Drizzle melted margarine over top. Bake at 450°F. about 15 minutes, until golden brown and crisp. Serves 4.
   Variation: Add 1 slice ham to the cheese in each sandwich.

Talking things out in the kitchen is much more natural than setting up a time and saying, "Now we will have a discussion."

JOHN L. THOMAS

TASTY CRACKER SPREAD

>   1 medium orange
>   1⅓ cups granola, crushed slightly
>   ¾ cup crunchy-style peanut butter
>   ¼ cup honey

1. Grate 1 teaspoon rind from orange.
2. Peel orange and chop it up.
3. Mix together in medium-size bowl the orange, orange rind, cereal, peanut butter, and honey.
4. Spread on crackers. Makes about 2 cups of topping.

8
Vegetables

FRENCH BEAN CASSEROLE

    2 **nine-ounce packages frozen, French-style green beans**
    1 **can cream of mushroom soup**
    ¼ **cup milk**
       dash of salt
    2 **tablespoons margarine**
    ½ **cup cornflakes, crushed to ¼ cup**

1. Using sharp knife, slice frozen beans crosswise into 1-inch lengths. Put in greased casserole dish.
2. Mix together soup, milk, and salt. Pour over beans.
3. Dot with margarine and sprinkle with crushed cornflakes.
4. Bake at 350°F. for about 60 minutes. Serves 8.
Variation: Substitute cream of chicken soup for cream of mushroom soup.

Be present at our table, Lord;
Be here, and everywhere, adored;
These mercies bless and grant that we
May strengthened for Thy service be.

BROCCOLI AND CORN AU GRATIN

¼ cup melted margarine
2 tablespoons all-purpose flour
¼ teaspoon salt
1½ cups milk
1½ cups (6 ounces) grated sharp cheddar cheese
1½ cups cornflakes, finely crushed to ¾ cup
1 can whole-kernel corn, drained
2 ten-ounce packages frozen broccoli spears,
   cooked and drained

1. Mix half of melted margarine with flour and salt. Gradually blend in milk, stirring until sauce is smooth and thickened.
2. Blend cheese into sauce. Add ¼ cup cereal crumbs and corn. Mix well.
3. Place broccoli in shallow baking dish. Pour cheese sauce on top.
4. Blend remaining crumbs and margarine and sprinkle over sauce.
5. Bake at 350°F. for 30 minutes. Serves 8.

CREAMY CORN PUDDING

1 can creamed corn
2 slightly beaten eggs
½ teaspoon salt
3 tablespoons melted margarine
1 cup cornflakes, crushed to ½ cup

1. Blend together creamed corn, eggs, and salt. Spoon into greased casserole.
2. Pour melted margarine over corn mixture. Sprinkle top with crushed cornflakes.
3. Bake at 350°F. for 30 to 35 minutes, until hot and bubbly. Serves 4 or 5.

Father, we thank Thee for the night
And for the pleasant morning light;
For rest and food and loving care,
And all that makes the world so fair.
AMEN.

BAKED CORN CUSTARD

2 tablespoons margarine
¼ cup chopped green pepper
1 small onion, finely chopped
3 eggs
2 cups milk
1 teaspoon salt
½ teaspoon sugar
⅛ teaspoon pepper
1 cup (4 ounces) shredded American cheese
1 can (1 pound) corn, drained
2 cups coarsely broken CORN CHEX cereal

1. Melt margarine in small saucepan. Add green pepper and onion, and cook until limp.
2. In medium-size bowl, beat together eggs, milk, salt, sugar, and pepper. Stir in cheese, corn, cooked green pepper and onion, and 1¾ cups cereal.
3. Pour corn mixture into 1½ quart casserole and top with remaining cereal.
4. Bake uncovered at 325°F. for 45 to 50 minutes, until set.
5. Cool 10 minutes before serving. Serves 6.

CRISP BAKED POTATO BALLS

1 egg, separated
½ teaspoon dried parsley flakes
1½ cups very stiff mashed potatoes, prepared with salt
1⅓ cups cornflakes, crushed to ⅔ cup
2 tablespoons melted margarine

1. Mix together egg yolk and parsley flakes. Blend in potatoes and mix thoroughly. Put aside.
2. Beat egg white until foamy. Put aside.
3. Measure level tablespoonfuls of potato mixture, and shape into balls.
4. Dip each ball in egg white, then roll in cereal crumbs.
5. Place in greased baking pan and drizzle melted margarine over top.
6. Bake at 450°F. about 10 minutes, until light brown. Makes 24 small potato balls. Serves 4 to 6.

God has given us two hands — one to receive with and the other to give with. We are not cisterns made for hoarding; we are channels made for sharing.   BILLY GRAHAM

BROCCOLI-POTATO BAKE

   4 cups CORN CHEX cereal, crushed to 2 cups
   ¼ cup melted margarine
   3 cups seasoned, hot mashed potatoes
   ½ cup dairy sour cream
   1 teaspoon dry, minced onion
   ¼ teaspoon seasoned salt
      dash of pepper
   1 ten-ounce package frozen, chopped broccoli, cooked and drained. Do not salt.
   1 cup grated American cheese

1. Grease 1½ quart casserole.
2. Mix cereal crumbs with margarine. Put aside.
3. Gently stir together potatoes, broccoli, sour cream, onion, salt, and pepper.
4. Spoon half of mixture into casserole. Top with half of cheese and half of crumbs. Repeat with remaining ingredients.
5. Bake at 350°F. until crumbs are golden brown, about 20 to 25 minutes. Serves about 8.

BROCCOLI-EGG CASSEROLE

3 cups RICE CHEX cereal, crushed to 1½ cups
1 teaspoon and 1 teaspoon seasoned salt
1 teaspoon dried, minced onion
6 tablespoons melted margarine
3 tablespoons flour
½ teaspoon dry mustard
2½ cups milk
1 teaspoon Worcestershire sauce
1 cup grated cheddar cheese
1 ten-ounce package frozen, chopped
    broccoli, cooked and drained
6 sliced, hard-cooked eggs

1. Mix together crushed cereal, 1 teaspoon seasoned salt, minced onion, and 2 tablespoons of the melted margarine. Put aside.
2. In medium-size saucepan, stir flour, 1 teaspoon seasoned salt, and mustard into remaining melted margarine. Add milk and Worcestershire sauce, stirring constantly. Cook until sauce is thickened.
3. Remove sauce from heat and blend in cheese. Gently stir in broccoli, sliced eggs, and 1 cup of crumb mixture. Place in shallow baking dish and top with remaining crumbs.
4. Bake at 350°F. until sauce is bubbly and top is browned, about 20 to 30 minutes. Serves 6.

How delightful is a timely word!   PROVERBS 15:23

CREAMY CARROT CASSEROLE

½ cup finely crushed cornflakes
5 tablespoons margarine
⅓ cup chopped onion
3 tablespoons flour
1 teaspoon salt
⅛ teaspoon pepper
1½ cups milk
1 cup shredded American cheese
4 cups sliced carrots, cooked and drained
1 tablespoon dried parsley flakes

1. Put cereal crumbs in small bowl. Melt 5 tablespoons margarine in large saucepan. Pour 2 tablespoons of the margarine over cereal. Mix well.
2. Cook onion in remaining margarine until onion is limp but not brown.
3. Add flour, salt, and pepper to onion mixture. Blend in milk, stirring constantly until thickened.
4. Stir cheese into sauce until it is melted and smooth. Take pan off heat.
5. Add carrots and parsley flakes to sauce. Pour mixture into 1½ quart, greased baking dish.
6. Sprinkle crumbs over top of carrots. Bake at 350°F. for about 20 minutes. Serves 8.

DELUXE CARROT RING

1 tablespoon shortening
2 cups cornflakes, crushed finely
  to ½ cup plus 2 tablespoons
1¾ cups cooked, mashed carrots
⅔ cup milk
1 cup grated sharp cheddar cheese
⅓ cup melted margarine
2 tablespoons finely chopped onion
¾ teaspoon salt
  dash of pepper
  dash of cayenne pepper
  dash of nutmeg
2 eggs
  parsley, for garnish

1. With shortening, grease a 1 quart ring mold. Sprinkle with 2 tablespoons crushed cereal.
2. Mix mashed carrots with remaining cereal, milk, cheese, margarine, onion, and seasonings.
3. Beat eggs with mixer until thickened. Blend into carrot mixture. Spoon into prepared mold.
4. Bake at 350°F. for 45 minutes, or until firm.
5. Remove from oven and cover with foil. Let stand 20 minutes. Unmold onto serving plate.
6. Garnish with parsley. Serves 6.

Variation: Fill center of ring with cooked peas.

A good laugh is sunshine in a house. WILLIAM MAKEPEACE THACKERAY

SCALLOPED CAULIFLOWER

   4 cups sliced cauliflower (1 medium-size head)
   2 tablespoons melted margarine
   ¼ teaspoon garlic salt
   ½ cup KELLOGG'S ALL-BRAN cereal
   1 chicken bouillon cube
   ¾ cup hot water
   ¼ cup margarine
   ¼ cup all-purpose flour
   ½ teaspoon salt
   ⅛ teaspoon pepper
   1 cup half-and-half
   2 tablespoons chopped pimiento
   ½ cup sliced green onions

1. Cook cauliflower just until tender. Drain liquid and put aside.
2. Meanwhile, mix together 2 tablespoons melted margarine, garlic salt, and cereal. Set aside for topping.
3. Dissolve bouillon cube in hot water and put aside.
4. In medium-size saucepan, melt ¼ cup margarine and stir in flour, salt, and pepper. Gradually add bouillon and half-and-half. Stir until thickened.
5. Blend cauliflower into sauce. Stir in pimiento and green onions. Pour mixture into 1½ quart, ungreased casserole. Top with crumb mixture.
6. Bake at 350°F. about 20 minutes. Serves 6 to 8.

SCALLOPED POTATOES AND ONIONS

5 tablespoons melted margarine
1 cup cornflakes, crushed to ½ cup
1½ cups thinly sliced onions
4½ cups thinly sliced, pared potatoes
1½ teaspoons salt
3 tablespoons all-purpose flour
¼ teaspoon pepper
¼ teaspoon paprika
1¾ cups milk

1. Mix 2 tablespoons melted margarine with crushed cornflakes. Save for topping.
2. In medium-size saucepan, cook onions and potatoes with 1 teaspoon salt in boiling water. Cook for 5 minutes and drain.
3. Combine flour with remaining margarine, remaining ½ teaspoon salt, and other seasonings. Add milk gradually to make a white sauce. Cook until thickened, stirring constantly.
4. Place ⅓ of the vegetables in a shallow casserole. Top with ⅓ of the sauce and repeat two times. Sprinkle with the reserved cereal topping mix.
5. Bake at 400°F. for 35 to 40 minutes, until tender. Serves 6 to 8.

Take care of your lambs, or where will you get your sheep from?

SPINACH CASSEROLE

   3 **tablespoons margarine**
   3 **cups RICE CHEX cereal, crushed to 1½ cups**
   1 **teaspoon dried, minced onion**
   1 **eight-ounce package cream cheese, softened**
   1 **thirteen-ounce can evaporated milk**
   2 **teaspoons lemon juice**
  ¾ **teaspoon seasoned salt**
      dash of white pepper
   1 **eight-ounce can sliced mushrooms,**
      drained (reserve ⅓ cup liquid)
   1 **well-beaten egg**
   1 **ten-ounce package frozen spinach,**
      cooked and drained

1. In small skillet, melt margarine. Add cereal and dried onion. Stir until cereal is coated. Put aside.

2. Combine softened cream cheese, milk, lemon juice, seasonings, and mushroom liquid in saucepan. Heat and stir until sauce is smooth.

3. Add beaten egg to sauce, and stir until thickened.

4. Stir in mushrooms and spinach, and pour mixture into shallow baking dish. Top with cereal mixture.

5. Bake at 350°F. until hot and topping is golden brown, about 20 minutes. Serves 8.

Better is a dish of vegetables where love is,
Than a fattened ox and hatred with it.

PROVERBS 15:17

ZUCCHINI CASSEROLE

    3 cups CORN CHEX cereal, crushed to 2 cups
    3 tablespoons melted margarine
    ¼ cup dry, grated Parmesan cheese
    1 can cream of chicken soup
    ¼ cup finely chopped onion
    2 tablespoons snipped parsley
    ¼ teaspoon salt
      dash white pepper
    6 cups thinly sliced, unpeeled zucchini
      paprika

1. Mix together cereal, melted margarine, and cheese. Put aside.
2. Mix together soup, onion, parsley, salt, and pepper.
3. Stir zucchini and ⅔ cup of cereal mixture into soup mixture. Pour into 1½ quart baking dish.
4. Top casserole with remaining cereal mixture. Sprinkle with paprika.
5. Bake uncovered at 350°F. about 30 minutes, until zucchini is tender and crumb topping is golden brown. Serves 6 to 8.

HEARTY VEGETABLE CASSEROLE

4 tablespoons margarine
2½ cups RICE CHEX cereal, crushed to 1½ cups
½ teaspoon thyme
1½ cups diced celery
1 tablespoon finely chopped onion
½ teaspoon salt
   dash pepper
1 can cream of mushroom soup
½ cup water
1½ cups cooked, sliced carrots, unseasoned
1½ cups cooked, cut green beans, unseasoned

1. Melt margarine in large skillet. Remove 2 tablespoons of the melted margarine and combine with the cereal and ¼ teaspoon of the thyme in a small bowl. Put aside.
2. Cook celery and onion in remaining margarine until vegetables are tender. Blend in salt, pepper, remaining ¼ teaspoon thyme, soup, and water. Mix well.
3. Stir cooked and drained carrots and green beans into sauce. Pour into 1½ quart casserole. Sprinkle cereal mixture over top.
4. Bake at 350°F. for about 30 minutes. Serves 6.

CRISPY FRIED MUSHROOMS

½ cup all-purpose flour
1 teaspoon salt
½ teaspoon baking powder
⅛ teaspoon pepper
1 egg, separated
1 teaspoon sugar
⅓ cup milk
1 pound washed mushrooms
5 cups CORN CHEX cereal, crushed to 1⅔ cups
shortening for frying

1. Mix together in small bowl the flour, salt, baking powder, and pepper.
2. Beat egg white until foamy. Sprinkle in sugar. Continue beating until peaks are stiff but still moist.
3. In medium-size bowl, beat egg yolk with milk. Add flour mixture gradually. Blend well. Fold in beaten egg white.
4. Dip mushrooms in batter. Let extra drip off. Roll in crushed cereal.
5. Deep fry in melted shortening at 385°F., until golden brown, turning once.
6. Drain on paper toweling, and salt as needed.

Children have more need of models than critics.   JOSEPH JANBERT

TOSSED SALAD

SALAD DRESSING
   1 **teaspoon salt**
   ¼ **teaspoon pepper**
   ½ **teaspoon dry mustard**
   3 **tablespoons vinegar**
   1 **tablespoon honey**
   ½ **cup vegetable oil**

SALAD TOPPING
   1 **tablespoon melted margarine**
   ¼ **teaspoon garlic salt**
   1 **tablespoon sunflower seeds**
   ¾ **cup KELLOGG'S RICE KRISPIES cereal**

SALAD
   4 **cups lettuce, torn into small pieces**
   4 **cups fresh spinach, torn into small pieces**
   3 **medium-size tomatoes, cut into wedges**

1. In small mixing bowl or blender, combine salt, pepper, dry mustard, vinegar, and honey. Gradually add oil while beating with mixer or mixing in blender. Refrigerate.
2. To melted margarine blend in garlic salt and sunflower seeds. Stir gently over low heat for a few seconds.
3. Stir cereal into seasoned margarine, coating well. Continue cooking and stirring until cereal is golden. Remove from heat, and let cool.
4. In salad bowl, toss together spinach and lettuce.
5. At serving time, toss together salad greens and tomato wedges. Mix in dressing. Put into individual salad bowls. Sprinkle cereal mixture over each salad.

SPINACH AND MUSHROOM SALAD

DRESSING
½ cup salad oil
¼ cup tarragon vinegar
1 teaspoon seasoned salt
½ teaspoon summer savory
¼ teaspoon pepper
1 small, thinly sliced onion
½ pound fresh mushrooms, cleaned and sliced

CROUTONS
3 tablespoons margarine
1 tablespoon Worcestershire sauce
1 minced garlic clove
2 cups CORN CHEX cereal
2 tablespoons sesame seeds

SPINACH
1 pound torn spinach

1. Mix dressing ingredients well. Let stand overnight in refrigerator.
2. Melt margarine and mix in Worcestershire sauce and garlic.
3. Stir in cereal and sesame seeds, coating evenly. Heat and stir over low heat 4 minutes, until lightly browned.
4. Remove cereal mixture from heat, and cool on paper toweling.
5. Wash spinach and drain well.
6. Place torn spinach in salad bowl and toss with dressing and croutons. Serves 6 to 8.

Older people's participation in our lives gives our children a sense of continuity — a sense of generations, of the flow and ebb of life. This perspective is one that children absorb: A realization that age means experience, that age need not be feared; a dim recognition that parents, too, were once children. Today we have suburban developments where children of young families are growing up without seeing old people as part of their day-to-day living. It seems to me that children need the natural balance of both young and old — and contact with their grand-parents helps to provide this. MRS. JONAS E. SALK

9
Holiday Foods

CRANBERRY COBBLER

- **2 cups bran flakes**
- **¾ cup firmly packed brown sugar**
- **½ cup all-purpose flour**
- **½ cup shredded coconut**
- **⅓ cup margarine**
- **1 tablespoon lemon juice**
- **2 cups (1-pound can) whole cranberry sauce**

1. In large mixing bowl, combine cereal, sugar, flour, and coconut.
2. With fork, cut in margarine until crumbly.
3. Press half the cereal mixture into greased 8 x 8 x 2 inch pan.
4. Stir lemon juice into cranberry sauce and spoon over tops of cereal mixture.
5. Top cranberries with other half of cereal mixture.
6. Bake at 350°F. about 40 minutes, until crisp and golden. Cut into squares. Serve warm with vanilla ice cream.

VALENTINE FLUFF

CRUMB MIXTURE
2 cups RICE CHEX cereal,
crushed to ¾ cup
2 tablespoons melted margarine
2 tablespoons firmly packed brown sugar
¼ cup chopped, toasted almonds

FILLING
1 four-ounce container
whipped topping
1 ten-ounce package frozen
strawberries in syrup, thawed

1. Brown cereal crumbs on cookie sheet at 300°F.
   about 10 minutes.
2. Mix together margarine, brown sugar, and almonds.
   Combine with cereal crumbs. Put aside while
   making filling.
3. Just before serving, fold whipped topping into strawberries.
   Alternate layers of strawberry filling and crumb mixture in
   parfait glasses or other dessert dishes. Serves 4 or 5.

BRAN-APPLE LOGS

1 cup chopped, dried apples
¾ cup chopped, candied fruit
4 cups BRAN CHEX cereal,
coarsely crushed
½ cup chopped nuts
¾ cup flaked coconut
1 three-and-three-quarter-ounce
package vanilla instant pudding mix
⅓ cup light corn syrup
1 tablespoon lemon juice

1. Combine fruits and crushed cereal in large bowl.
2. Add nuts and ½ cup coconut to cereal mixture.
3. Mix together dry pudding mix, corn syrup, and lemon
   juice.
4. Pour pudding mixture over cereal mixture. Mix well.
5. Form mixture into 2 rolls, 1½ inches in diameter and
   about 6 inches long. Roll logs in ¼ cup coconut.
6. Wrap logs in plastic wrap. Freeze. Slice while frozen into
   ¼-inch slices. Makes about 4 dozen slices.

CHEESE BALL

2 three-ounce packages softened cream cheese
¼ cup (2 ounces) bleu cheese
⅓ cup (3 ounces) process cheese spread
1 tablespoon grated onion
½ teaspoon Worcestershire sauce
1 cup KELLOGG'S CRACKLIN' BRAN cereal,
**   crushed to ¾ cup**
¼ cup chopped pecans
3 tablespoons parsley flakes

1. Mix together the cheeses, onion, and Worcestershire sauce. Blend well.
2. Add ½ cup crushed cereal, nuts, and 2 tablespoons parsley flakes to the cheese mixture. Mix well.
3. Cover and chill in refrigerator for 4 hours or overnight.
4. Combine remaining ¼ cup cereal crumbs with parsley flakes.
5. About 1 hour before serving, mold cheese into a ball and roll in cereal mixture. Store in refrigerator. Serve with crackers.

Deserved applause with love is the kind of buildup every grandchild needs.   CATHARINE BRANDT

GRILLED BANANAS

1 egg
½ teaspoon salt
2 tablespoons brown sugar
4 green-tipped bananas, peeled
2 cups cornflakes, crushed
¼ cup melted margarine

1. Beat egg slightly. Stir in salt and sugar.
2. Dip bananas into egg mixture, then in crushed cereal.
3. Grill bananas on large piece of aluminum foil, 2 to 3 inches from hot coals.
4. Baste bananas with melted margarine as they cook. Turn once. Takes 8 to 12 minutes for fruit to be hot and cereal to brown lightly. Serves 4.
   Variation: These can be broiled indoors about 8 inches from heat.

The finest autobiography any man can write is little words of kindness stored up in a loved one's heart.

PEPPERMINT REFRIGERATOR DESSERT

CRUST
2 cups GOLDEN GRAHAMS breakfast
cereal, crushed
¼ cup honey
2 tablespoons melted margarine

FILLING
24 regular marshmallows
½ cup milk
1 teaspoon vanilla
⅛ teaspoon salt
6 drops peppermint extract
6 drops red food coloring
2 cups whipped cream or
nondairy whipped topping

CANDY TOPPING
2 tablespoons crushed
peppermint candy

1. Mix crushed cereal with honey and melted margarine.
2. Spoon crumb mixture into 8-inch square pan. Press firmly to form crust. Chill.
3. In heavy saucepan, melt marshmallows in milk. Add vanilla, salt, peppermint extract, and red coloring.
4. Remove pan from heat, and cool in pan of cold water. Stir while it cools and begins to thicken.
5. Fold marshmallow mixture into whipped cream, and spoon onto crust. Wrap and chill overnight.
6. Just before serving, top with crushed candy and cut into squares. Serves 9.

If you make children happy now, you will make them happy twenty years hence by the memory of it.   KATE DOUGLAS WIGGIN

CHERRY REFRIGERATOR DESSERT

   3 cups GOLDEN GRAHAMS breakfast cereal, crushed
¼ cup melted margarine
   1 cup chilled whipping cream
   1 three-ounce package cream cheese, softened
½ cup sugar
   1 teaspoon vanilla
   1 cup miniature marshmallows
   1 twenty-one ounce can cherry pie filling, chilled

1. Combine cereal and melted margarine. Press into bottom of ungreased 8 x 8 x 2 inch pan.
2. Whip cream in chilled bowl until stiff.
3. In another bowl, beat cream cheese, sugar, and vanilla until fluffy.
4. Fold whipped cream and miniature marshmallows into cheese mixture.
5. Chill in refrigerator at least 4 hours. Spread cherry pie filling over top. Serves 9.
   Variation: For a blueberry dessert, substitute 1 can blueberry pie filling for the cherry pie filling.

RASPBERRY TARTS

CRUST
   2 tablespoons margarine
  20 large or 2 cups miniature
     marshmallows
  ¼ teaspoon vanilla
  2½ cups KELLOGG'S RICE KRISPIES cereal

FILLING
   1 cup whipping cream
   2 tablespoons sugar
   1 ten-ounce package frozen
     raspberries, thawed, well drained

1. Melt margarine in large saucepan. Stir in marshmallows and cook over low heat until melted and blended.
2. Remove from heat and mix in vanilla and cereal. Stir well.
3. Form tarts by dividing mixture into 8 parts and pressing into large custard cups or muffin cups. Let set until firm.
4. Whip cream and sugar together until soft peaks form. Carefully stir in drained fruit.
5. Spoon into tarts. Garnish with additional berries.
   Variations: Substitute strawberries, peaches, or blueberries for raspberries.
   Use whipped topping in place of whipped cream.

We may give without loving, but we cannot love without giving.

CHRISTMAS DATE BALLS

½ cup margarine
¾ cup sugar
1 pound pitted dates,
  cut up (2½ cups)
1 well-beaten egg
1 tablespoon milk
½ teaspoon salt
1 teaspoon vanilla
½ cup chopped nuts
4 cups WHEATIES breakfast cereal,
  crushed to make 2 cups
  finely chopped nuts or coconut

1. Combine margarine, sugar, and dates in medium-size, heavy saucepan. Cook over low heat, stirring constantly, until margarine is melted. Remove from heat.
2. Combine beaten egg, milk, salt, and vanilla. Stir into date mixture.
3. Cook over very low heat, stirring constantly, about 4 minutes, until dates are soft and ingredients are well mixed.
4. Stir in nuts. Cool 5 minutes.
5. Stir in cereal. When cool enough to handle, shape into small balls. Roll in chopped nuts or coconut.
   Makes 50 to 70.

Great gifts can be given by little hands,
Since of all gifts Love is still the best.   ADELAIDE PROCTER

CHERRY JEWELS

  ⅓ **cup shortening**
  ½ **cup sugar**
  1 **teaspoon grated lemon peel**
  1 **egg**
  2 **tablespoons milk**
  1 **teaspoon vanilla**
  1 **cup sifted all-purpose flour**
  ½ **teaspoon baking powder**
  ¼ **teaspoon baking soda**
  ¼ **teaspoon salt**
  ½ **cup chopped walnuts**
  ½ **cup raisins or chopped dates**
1½ **cups WHEATIES breakfast cereal, slightly crushed candied cherries**

1. Cream together shortening, sugar, and lemon peel. Beat in egg and mix well.
2. Stir in milk and vanilla.
3. Sift together flour, baking powder, soda, and salt. Add to creamed mixture and mix well.
4. Stir nuts and raisins or dates into dough.
5. Lightly form balls of dough with teaspoon, and roll in crushed cereal to coat.
6. Place cookies 2 inches apart on greased baking sheets. Top each with portion of cherry.
7. Bake at 400°F. for 12 minutes. Cool slightly before removing to wire rack. Makes 3 dozen cookies.

Children need love, especially when they do not deserve it.
                                  HAROLD S. HULBERT

SNOWMAN

¼ cup margarine
1 ten-ounce package (about
   40 regular) marshmallows
½ teaspoon vanilla
½ cup chopped, candied cherries
½ cup coarsely chopped pecans
5 cups KELLOGG'S RICE KRISPIES cereal
   gumdrops

1. Melt margarine and marshmallows in large saucepan over low heat, stirring to blend.
2. Remove from heat and stir in vanilla.
3. Add cherries, nuts, and cereal, stirring to coat evenly.
4. While warm, shape into 3 balls and form a snowman. Decorate with gumdrops.
   Variation: Form into balls and roll in coconut or colored sugar.

CHERRY-DATE DELIGHTS

¾ cup softened margarine
1 cup sugar
2 eggs
1 teaspoon vanilla
2 tablespoons milk
2¼ cups all-purpose flour
2 teaspoons baking powder
½ teaspoon salt
1 cup chopped nuts
1 cup finely cut, pitted dates
⅓ cup finely chopped maraschino cherries
2⅔ cups cornflakes, crushed to 1⅓ cups

1. In large bowl, cream margarine and sugar together until light.
2. Add eggs and vanilla. Beat well and add milk.
3. Sift together flour, baking powder, and salt. Add to creamed mixture. Mix well.
4. Stir in chopped nuts, dates, and cherries.
5. Using teaspoon, shape dough into small balls. Roll in crushed cereal and place on greased cookie sheets about 2 inches apart.
6. Top each cookie with piece of cherry and bake at 375°F. about 10 minutes. Makes about 5 dozen cookies.

KIX CHRISTMAS TREES

¼ cup margarine
½ pound (about 40 regular) marshmallows
5 cups KIX breakfast cereal
10 wooden skewers
    green sugar
10 large gumdrops

1. Melt margarine and marshmallows in large saucepan over low heat, stirring to blend.
2. Remove from heat and stir in cereal. Press into greased, cone-shaped drinking cups. Press skewer in center of each for tree trunk.
3. When set, remove paper. Roll in green sugar.
4. Push bottom of each skewer into large gumdrop. Makes 10 trees.

And these words, which I am commanding you today,...you shall teach them diligently to your sons.   DEUTERONOMY 6:6-7

RASPBERRY GEMS

1½ cups all-purpose flour
2 tablespoons cornstarch
½ cup unsifted confectioners' sugar
1 cup softened margarine
1¾ cups granola
½ cup raspberry jam

1. Combine flour, cornstarch, and sugar. With fork, mix in margarine to form soft dough.
2. Cover mixture and refrigerate at least 30 minutes.
3. Shape mixture into small balls. Roll in cereal. Place about 2 inches apart on ungreased cookie sheets.
4. Use ½ teaspoon measuring spoon to make indentation in center of each ball.
5. Bake at 350°F. for 5 minutes. Press measuring spoon into centers again. Bake an additional 5 to 7 minutes, until light brown. Remove from oven and fill each center with ½ teaspoon jam. Makes about 3 dozen cookies.

SHERRY'S GRANDMA'S SKILLET COOKIES

      5 tablespoons butter or margarine
    1½ cups chopped dates
      1 cup sugar
      ¼ teaspoon salt
      2 beaten eggs
      1 teaspoon vanilla
      ½ cup flaked coconut
    2½ cups crushed KELLOGG'S RICE KRISPIES cereal

1. Melt butter or margarine in large skillet over low heat.
2. Mix in chopped dates, sugar, salt, beaten eggs, and vanilla.
   Cook, stirring constantly, until well blended. Add coconut.
   Cool slightly.
3. Stir in 2 cups of the crushed cereal. Shape into balls. Roll
   in remaining crushed cereal. Set on waxed paper. Chill.
   Makes 3 to 4 dozen cookies.
   Variation: Add ½ cup chopped nuts and ½ cup candied
   fruit. Roll in flaked coconut instead of crushed cereal.

---

*What your young people learn today determines what the church will
know tomorrow.*   HENRIETTA C. MEARS

COOKIE WREATH

      ⅓ cup margarine
      1 ten-ounce package (about 40 regular
        or 4 cups miniature) marshmallows
      1 teaspoon green food coloring
      ½ teaspoon vanilla
      6 cups cornflakes
        red cinnamon candies

1. Melt margarine and marshmallows in large saucepan
   over low heat, stirring to blend.
2. Remove from heat. Add food coloring and vanilla.
3. Stir cereal into green mixture until evenly coated.
4. Spoon warm mixture into 1½ quart, buttered ring mold
   and press firmly.
5. While still warm, unmold onto plate and decorate with
   red candies.
6. When cool, slice to serve. Makes 30 1-inch slices.
   Variation: Shape into 12 small wreaths instead of 1 large
   one. Decorate each with cinnamon candies.

CHEX CHRISTMAS STAR

   3 **tablespoons margarine**
3½ **cups miniature marshmallows**
   6 **cups RICE CHEX cereal, crushed to 4 cups**
  ⅓ **cup chopped, red and green**
     candied cherries
  ⅓ **cup chopped nuts**

1. Melt margarine and marshmallows in large saucepan over low heat, stirring to blend.
2. Remove from heat and add cereal, candied fruit, and nuts.
3. With buttered hands, press into greased star mold or shape into star with hands.

One of the lovely ways of making Christmas the glowing occasion it should be is to use it as a special time for kind deeds.

ELIZABETH WALKER STRACHAN

TUTTI FRUTTI COOKIES

1¾ **cups all-purpose flour**
 ½ **teaspoon baking soda**
 ½ **teaspoon salt**
  2 **cups KELLOGG'S PRODUCT 19 cereal,**
    crushed to 1 cup
  1 **cup softened margarine**
  1 **cup sugar**
 ½ **cup firmly packed brown sugar**
  1 **egg**
  1 **teaspoon vanilla**
  1 **cup finely cut, mixed**
    candied fruit

1. Sift flour, soda, and salt together in small bowl. Stir in crushed cereal.
2. In large bowl, cream together margarine and sugars. Beat in egg and vanilla. Gradually add flour mixture, stirring well. Fold in candied fruit.
3. Drop dough by teaspoonfuls onto ungreased cookie sheets. Bake at 350°F. for 12 to 15 minutes, until lightly browned. Cool slightly before placing on racks.
Makes 3 to 4 dozen cookies.

Those who bring sunshine into the lives of others cannot keep it from themselves.
                                                                J. M. BARRIE

HOLIDAY CHERRY COOKIES

1½ **cups flour**
½ **teaspoon salt**
½ **teaspoon baking soda**
½ **teaspoon baking powder**
½ **cup softened margarine**
1 **cup and 3 tablespoons sugar**
1 **egg**
½ **teaspoon almond extract**
2 **cups RICE CHEX cereal, crushed to 1 cup**
½ **cup chopped, green and red candied cherries**

1. Sift together flour, salt, soda, and baking powder.
2. Cream margarine with 1 cup sugar. Mix in egg and almond extract.
3. Stir flour mixture into creamed mixture, blending well. Fold in cereal and cherries.
4. Shape mixture into small balls. Roll in remaining 3 tablespoons sugar.
5. Place on cookie sheets, about 2 inches apart. Bake at 375°F. 8 to 10 minutes, until light brown on bottom. Cool on rack. Makes about 5 dozen cookies.

HOLIDAY SNACK MIX

½ cup margarine
1 tablespoon Worcestershire sauce
¼ teaspoon celery salt
¼ teaspoon seasoned salt
¼ teaspoon cayenne
¼ teaspoon onion salt
¼ teaspoon garlic salt
1 cup CHEERIOS breakfast cereal
2 cups RICE CHEX cereal
2 cups WHEAT CHEX cereal
2 cups CORN CHEX cereal
1 cup very thin pretzel sticks
½ cup peanuts or slivered almonds

1. Melt margarine in large, shallow baking pan. Blend in Worcestershire sauce and seasonings.
2. Stir cereals, pretzels, and nuts into seasoned margarine.
3. Bake mixture for 1 hour at 250°F. Stir every 5 to 10 minutes.
4. Cool completely. Store in covered container in cool place. Makes about 8 cups.
   Variation: Fill gift casserole or other container with this snack mix. Gift wrap.

FOURTH OF JULY HAMBURGERS

  1 **slightly beaten egg**
  1 **tablespoon minced onion**
1½ **teaspoons Worcestershire sauce**
  ¾ **teaspoon salt**
  ¾ **teaspoon chili powder**
  2 **tablespoons barbecue sauce**
1½ **cups WHEAT CHEX cereal,**
    crushed to ½ cup
1½ **pounds lean ground beef**

1. Mix egg, onion, Worcestershire sauce, salt, chili powder, and barbecue sauce in large bowl.
2. Add crushed cereal and meat. Mix well.
3. Form 6 patties. Broil or grill 8 to 12 minutes, depending on desired degree of doneness. Turn once while cooking. Brush with additional barbecue sauce, if desired.

A child's heart
  Is freshly turned earth
Fertile and waiting
For the seed of truth...
The gentle rain of faith...
The warmth of love.
A child's heart
  Is freshly turned earth.
What we plant
Is reaped
For good or bad...
Life giving grain
Or tangled weeds.

WANDA STURGILL VAIL

Index

CHRISTIAN HERALD ASSOCIATION AND ITS MINISTRIES

CHRISTIAN HERALD ASSOCIATION, founded in 1878, publishes The Christian Herald Magazine, one of the leading interdenominational religious monthlies in America. Through its wide circulation, it brings inspiring articles and the latest news of religious developments to many families. From the magazine's pages came the initiative for CHRISTIAN HERALD CHILDREN'S HOME and THE BOWERY MISSION, two individually supported not-for-profit corporations.

CHRISTIAN HERALD CHILDREN'S HOME, established in 1894, is the name for a unique and dynamic ministry to disadvantaged children, offering hope and opportunities which would not otherwise be available for reasons of poverty and neglect. The goal is to develop each child's potential and to demonstrate Christian compassion and understanding to children in need.

Mont Lawn is a permanent camp located in Bushkill, Pennsylvania. It is the focal point of a ministry which provides a healthful "vacation with a purpose" to children who without it would be confined to the streets of the city. Up to 1000 children between the ages of 7 and 11 come to Mont Lawn each year.

Christian Herald Children's Home maintains year-round contact with children by means of an *In-City Youth Ministry*. Central to its philosophy is the belief that only through sustained relationships and demonstrated concern can individual lives be truly enriched. Special emphasis is on individual guidance, spiritual and family counseling and tutoring. This follow-up ministry to inner-city children culminates for many in financial assistance toward higher education and career counseling.

THE BOWERY MISSION, located at 227 Bowery, New York City, has since 1879 been reaching out to the lost men on the Bowery, offering them what could be their last chance to rebuild their lives. Every man is fed, clothed and ministered to. Countless numbers have entered the 90-day residential rehabilitation program at the Bowery Mission. A concentrated ministry of counseling, medical care, nutrition therapy, Bible study and Gospel services awakens a man to spiritual renewal within himself.

These ministries are supported solely by the voluntary contributions of individuals and by legacies and bequests. Contributions are tax deductible. Checks should be made out either to CHRISTIAN HERALD CHILDREN'S HOME or to THE BOWERY MISSION.

Administrative Office: 40 Overlook Drive, Chappaqua, New York 10514
Telephone: (914) 769-9000